HARLEY MEMORABILIA

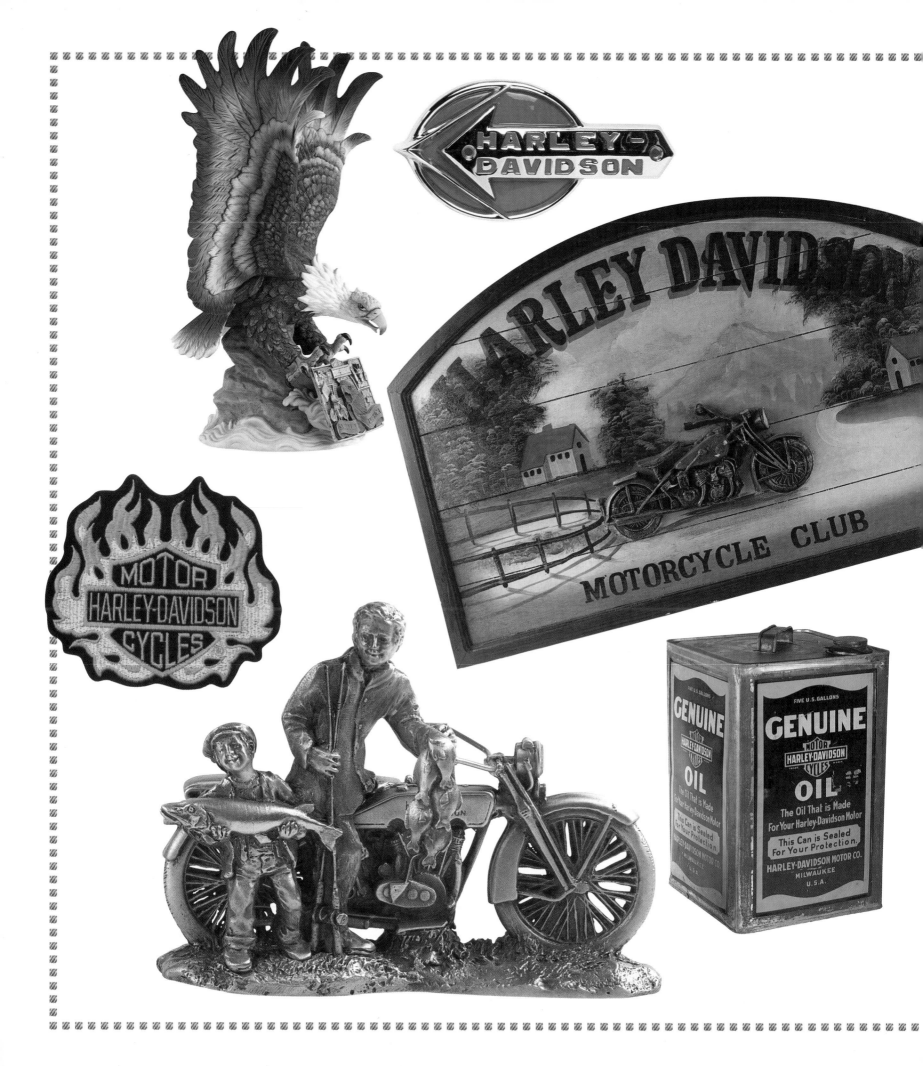

HARLEY MEMORABILIA

An Illustrated Guide to Harley-Davidson® Accessories, Mementos and Collectibles

TOD RAFFERTY

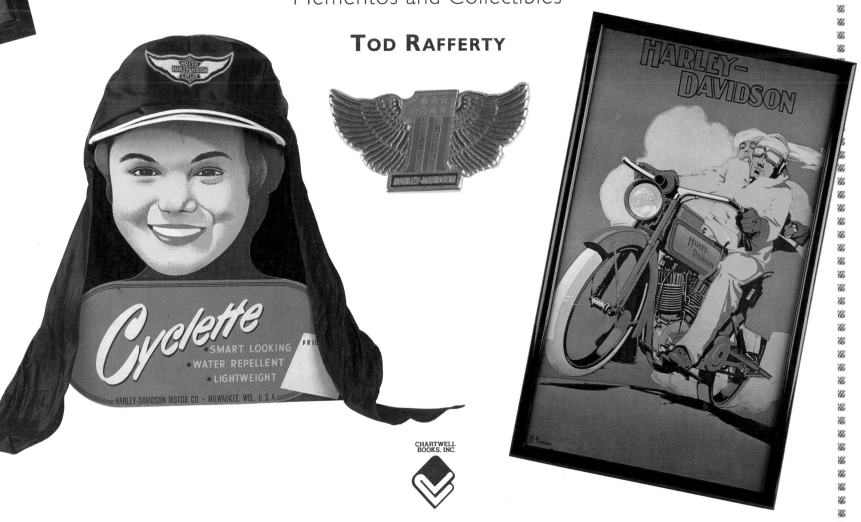

CHARTWELL BOOKS, INC.

CHARTWELL BOOKS
A division of Book Sales, Inc.
114 Northfield Avenue,
Edison, N.J. 08837, USA

CLB 4951
© 1997 CLB International,
Godalming, Surrey, UK

ISBN 0-7858-0821-3

The information in this book is true and
complete to the best of our knowledge. All
recommendations are made without any
guarantee on the part of the author or
publisher, who also disclaim any liability
incurred in connection with the use of
these data or specific details.

The name Harley-Davidson® and certain
model designations are the properties of
the trademark holder. They are used
herein only for the purposes of
identification. This is not an official Harley-
Davidson publication

CREDITS

Editor: Philip de Ste. Croix

Designer: Jill Coote

Photographer: Neil Sutherland

Production: Ruth Arthur, Sally Connolly,
Neil Randles, Paul Randles, Karen Staff

Director of production: Gerald Hughes

Color reproduction: Advance Laser
Graphic Arts, Hong Kong

Printed and bound in Spain by
Graficromo S.A.

THE AUTHOR

Tod Rafferty has been riding and racing motorcycles for 35 years. His previous
books are *Harley Davidson: The Ultimate Machine* (Running Press 1994) and *The
Complete Harley-Davidson* (Motorbooks International 1997). He is currently
working on an illustrated history of Indian motorcycles. Rafferty and his family live
on the central coast of California.

CONTENTS

INTRODUCTION

THIS book is full of motorcycling memories. These mementos appear in homes, shops, garages and dealerships around the country, in a variety of forms. The collectors' walls and display cases hold posters, books, magazines, banners, patches, pins, medallions, clocks, watches, toys, motorcycle parts, accessories, lubricants, signs, cans, bottles, steins, knives, trophies, trinkets, models, photographs, programs, decals, postcards, paintings, sculpture, belts, boots, badges, bags, banks, plates, ornaments and assorted sundries.

Most of the pieces shown here represent Harley-Davidson motomobilia, though some are more generic artifacts from the American Motorcycle Association, regional clubs and motorcycle dealers. But what they hold in common is the shared experience of motorcycling history, and each collector's favorite symbols and images. Plus the personal records of the individual's participation in the everlasting ride.

These timelines to the past are often sprinkled with the antique patina of quaint nostalgia, others are simple souvenirs of times and travels passed. But together they fill the framework of a great mural illustrating the history of motorcycling in the USA. This storyboard is crowded with detail, description and imagery of the sport's early heroes and heroines. The setting includes all the hardware, costumes, jewelry, advertising, banners, booklets and nick-nacks commemorating the evolution of American motorcycling.

And the faces in this panoramic portrait of two-wheeled history look out at us from the distant reaches of memory and biography, which but for these mementos would otherwise fade. Notice that most of the faces are smiling, as if to say, "Have a good ride."

SUGGESTED RETAIL

Assigning dollar values to some of these items is a dodgy enterprise. Many objects are simply not for sale, so pricing becomes a matter of speculation. In most cases the owners themselves have provided the amounts, based not necessarily on what they may sell the pieces for, but on what similar items bring in the marketplace.

We have attempted to reach a rough consensus by averaging the owners' estimates and figures published in several books on motorcycle collectibles. Some artifacts may be found for considerably less then the prices shown here. And some for quite a bit more. But like mementos from any sport or pastime, motomobilia prices hinge on rarity and condition. Limited numbers and original condition mean higher prices. And vice-versa.

So the prices cited represent a range from fair to excellent condition, and are listed following each description. Where the original price is known, the entry shows that followed by the current range: ($5/50-100), or by the current value range, ($100-150). If neither the original price nor current value is known, no price ($ np) is given.

Tod Rafferty
Atascadero,
California
1997

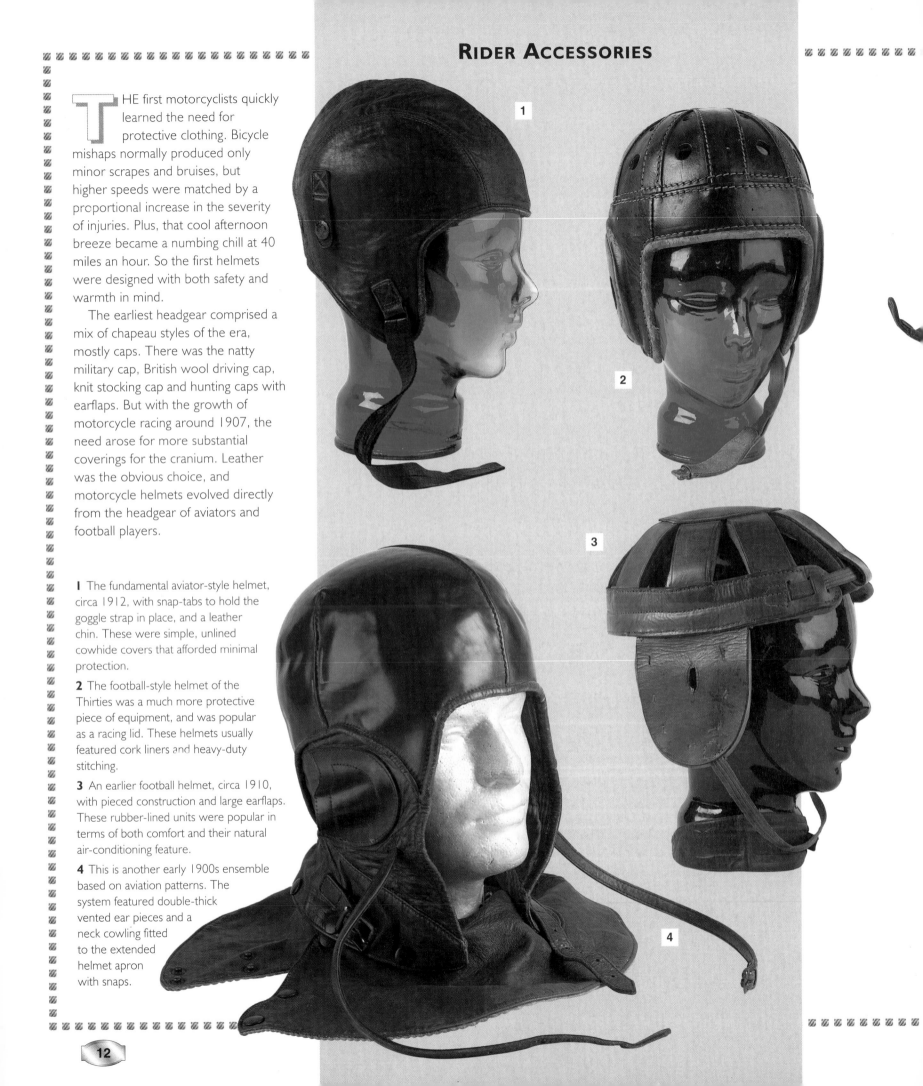

THE first motorcyclists quickly learned the need for protective clothing. Bicycle mishaps normally produced only minor scrapes and bruises, but higher speeds were matched by a proportional increase in the severity of injuries. Plus, that cool afternoon breeze became a numbing chill at 40 miles an hour. So the first helmets were designed with both safety and warmth in mind.

The earliest headgear comprised a mix of chapeau styles of the era, mostly caps. There was the natty military cap, British wool driving cap, knit stocking cap and hunting caps with earflaps. But with the growth of motorcycle racing around 1907, the need arose for more substantial coverings for the cranium. Leather was the obvious choice, and motorcycle helmets evolved directly from the headgear of aviators and football players.

1 The fundamental aviator-style helmet, circa 1912, with snap-tabs to hold the goggle strap in place, and a leather chin. These were simple, unlined cowhide covers that afforded minimal protection.

2 The football-style helmet of the Thirties was a much more protective piece of equipment, and was popular as a racing lid. These helmets usually featured cork liners and heavy-duty stitching.

3 An earlier football helmet, circa 1910, with pieced construction and large earflaps. These rubber-lined units were popular in terms of both comfort and their natural air-conditioning feature.

4 This is another early 1900s ensemble based on aviation patterns. The system featured double-thick vented ear pieces and a neck cowling fitted to the extended helmet apron with snaps.

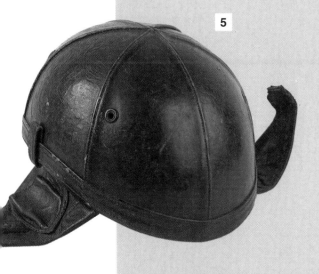

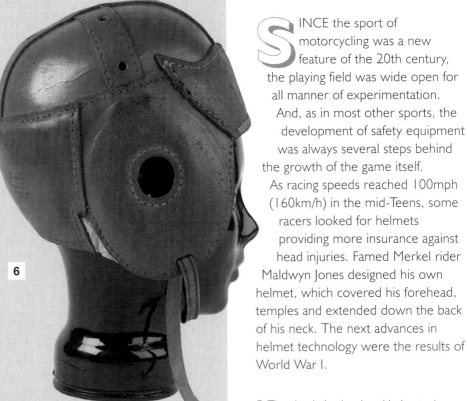

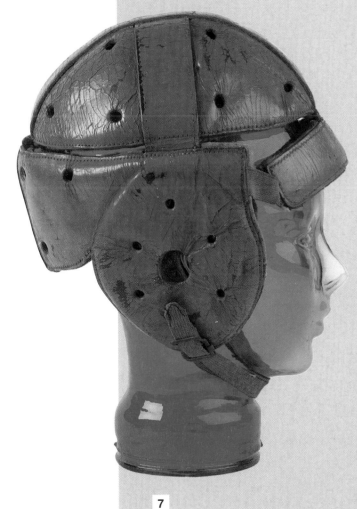

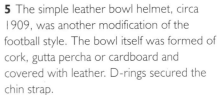

S INCE the sport of motorcycling was a new feature of the 20th century, the playing field was wide open for all manner of experimentation. And, as in most other sports, the development of safety equipment was always several steps behind the growth of the game itself.

As racing speeds reached 100mph (160km/h) in the mid-Teens, some racers looked for helmets providing more insurance against head injuries. Famed Merkel rider Maldwyn Jones designed his own helmet, which covered his forehead, temples and extended down the back of his neck. The next advances in helmet technology were the results of World War I.

5 The simple leather bowl helmet, circa 1909, was another modification of the football style. The bowl itself was formed of cork, gutta percha or cardboard and covered with leather. D-rings secured the chin strap.

6 The unit-construction football styles of the Twenties incorporated double-layer leather pads at the front and rear, ventilation holes at the top and large ear holes, so the engine (or the quarterback) was audible.

7 This football derivation features three-piece construction, with straps holding the two lower sections to the crown. Ventilation was given almost equal consideration as protection on this model.

8 Another aviator style, this helmet incorporates a built-in goggle assembly affixed by three snaps. Two snaps on the chin strap offer some measure of adjustment.

Prices: Vintage helmet prices vary widely according to age, condition, authenticity and style. Current prices range from $50 to $600.

(All helmets courtesy of Dale Walksler's Wheels Through Time Museum, Mt. Vernon, Illinois).

VISIBILITY and eye protection were among the first concerns of early motorcyclists.

Just as the first riding helmets followed aviation designs, motorcycle goggles took similar forms. Leather and canvas were the foremost materials for the construction of both helmets and goggles. Cranial protection ran a distant third to warmth and comfort, though racers soon adopted football helmets for a greater measure of safety.

1 The miraculous Turbo Visor appeared in the early Sixties. Though not associated with Harley-Davidson in particular, the Flash Gordon design influence made it a novelty item and therefore a certain collectible. The centrifugal rain shield was made by the Shinwa Company of Japan. ($30-75). (Bill's Custom Cycles).

2 The display case for Willson Goggles featured a broad range of styles and prices. From heavy duty spectatcles to round, rectangular and teardrop lenses, the early riders were offered a reasonable selection of shapes and types of goggles. The technology push provided by World War I ("mechanized warfare" was the new term) came to benefit motorcyclists in peacetime. As motorcycle speeds increased, so did the need for eye protectors that repelled most of the wind, dust and smoke intrinsic to open motoring. ($ np). (Wheels Through Time Museum).

HELMETS designed specifically for motorcycling gained more acceptance in the late Teens. By the early Twenties a number of manufacturers had noticed the market potential offered by motorcyclists, and undertook the building of helmets with features addressing riders' needs. The development of motorcycle goggles followed a similar path, showing more specialized forms as the motorcycle sport grew more firmly established.

3 Genuine Harley-Davidson shatter-proof goggles were first offered in the early Twenties. The eyepieces attached to a sheepskin backing, and fitted to the head with an elastic band. ($200-300). (Pat and Al Doerman collection).

4 The canvas helmet appeared in the Harley-Davidson catalog in the mid-Teens, and in this version offered some neck protection. The hinged goggles feature a cotton and sheepskin backing and elastic band. ($100-150). (Wheels Through Time Museum).

5 Clockwise from top:
The A-N racing goggles were stoutly built with a heavy-duty hinge, and offered good peripheral vision. Leather backing conformed to the face to seal out dust. ($100-200).
The blue-lensed Indian Rocket goggles were among the first to use foam rubber as a foundation. ($100-200).
The sun-baked eyepieces on the right bore no identification, but appear to be an early military style. ($100-200).
The unlined leather aviator helmet is pictured with a pair of Luxor goggles manufactured by G.B. Meyrowitz. ($100-200). (Wheels Through Time Museum).

COVERINGS for craniums remained a mix of style and function for decades. Then as now, many riders shunned the notion that motorcycling required a hard-shell covering for the skull. Comfort was a more important consideration, and the element of style could certainly not be ignored. The well-outfitted rider was expected to display a commanding presence on the roadway, to present a strong and distinctive appearance to match the bold and adventurous nature of the sport.

1 Harley-Davidson cotton denim headgear with goggle strap holders and company logo, circa 1926. These were standard mild-weather cranium covers that were basically aviator helmet liners. ($50-75). (Wheels Through Time Museum).

2 Contemporary baseball caps manufactured under license from Harley-Davidson. Prices range from $14-17. (The Shop).

3 Military-style caps in brushed cotton and natty corduroy, circa 1936. These caps were popular with motorcycle clubs, which often used their own insignias on the front. They sold originally for $2-3. Originals in good shape now sell for $50-200. The same style is still offered by Milwaukee. (Bill's Custom Cycles).

4

5

6

HARD-SHELL motorcycle helmets remained exceptions to the rule from the Twenties through the Fifties. Motorcycling fashions, while hardly original in the sport's early days, developed from military and police garments of the era. Durability, comfort and style was the order of priority, and with the advent of synthetic fabrics the range and quality of purpose-built motorcycle wear grew accordingly.

Harley-Davidson was among the first manufacturers to exploit motorcycle clothing for advertising purposes. The popularity of racing in the late Teens provided Milwaukee with convincing evidence that heros wearing the Harley logo had significant influence among potential customers, and with fans who already owned Milwaukee iron. So clothing and accessories, prominently marked with the company brand, were and are a prominent concern at Harley-Davidson.

4 Harley-Davidson skull cap with ear flaps, lined with fur. This mountain-man style was popular with hardy riders in the snow belt. This cap was first offered in the late Twenties. ($75-125). (Wheels Through Time Museum).

5 The beanie in Harley racing colors was a popular with racers, mechanics and railbirds in the Sixties. ($10-30). (Mark George collection).

6 The Cyclette cap was aimed at women riders and passengers of the Fifties. The foreign legion apron helped protect the ladies' hair from the effects of wind and road grime. ($100-150). (Wheels Through Time Museum).

MILWAUKEE'S emphasis on brand identification, prominently displayed, was not lost on their dealers around the country. As the motorcycle market grew more competitive with the influx of British and European brands, Harley-Davidson dealers took new interest in flying the corporate flag.

Few serious dealerships went without their own T-shirts in the Fifties, and more astute marketing types expanded the roster to put the company name on caps, jackets and coats. Many dealers created their own patches, which could be sewn on the customer's garment of choice. And the growing popularity of leather jackets and vests offered dealers a durable billboard upon which to display both the corporate emblem and their own business names.

1 T-shirt and handbag from Swim's Harley-Davidson shop in Energy, Illinois, circa 1950. ($ np).

2 This official Harley-Davidson shop coat, circa 1940, was made by Protexall of Galesburg, Illinois. ($200-250).

3 The wool knit shirt was a staple in the motorcyclist's wardrobe. This zippered turtleneck was a product of the early Forties. ($250-300). The navy-style cap features the H-D winged logo and assorted AMA pins. ($100-150).

4 Harley-Davidson coveralls were standard issue for shop mechanics in the Forties. ($150-200).

MOTORCYCLE togs continued to display the influence of styles from both the military and racing realms. The clothing of both disciplines proved well adapted to the rigors of motorcyling, since it was generally designed and constructed to withstand considerable abuse and exhibit some measure of durability.

The fashion element was something of an added bonus for civilian motorcyclists, who could easily adopt the demeanor of soldier or athlete without the attendant hazards of hostile fire or brutish competitors. As motorcycle factions multiplied in the Fifties, the apparel began to reflect new distinctions among riders with specific attitudes about the sport. Black leather jackets, T-shirts, vests and headbands came to symbolize one social category, military and police-style uniforms another, and sport riders in one-piece leathers another altogether. The costumes were a changin'.

5 Military-style puttees, traditional army garb of World War I, were still made in the Forties by the Keystone C&A Manufacturing Company. ($35-75).

6 The stylish rider of the Forties might sport a nylon racing jersey, studded leather kidney belt, gabardine trousers and knee-high Wellington boots. Ready for the Sunday ride. ($350-500).

7 Racing-style wool jerseys held wide popularity for motorcyclists, offering warmth and freedom of movement. They were equally popular with moths. ($ np).

(All clothing courtesy of Wheels Through Time Museum, Mt. Vernon, Illinois.)

PRIOR to the Fifties, motorcycle suspension was marginal. Harley-Davidson's seatpost spring was effective, but severely cobbled roads still delivered their rough edges to the rider. The first kidney belts were designed primarily with back support in mind; the fact that they also constrained the abrupt movement of several vital internal organs was just a bonus.

The majority of contemporary motorcycling of the era was conducted on fairly smooth roads at moderate speeds. But after several hours in the saddle, no matter how comfortable the perch, the lower back muscles could grow severely irritated. So bracing the back and spine against an unnaturally curved profile was an effective way to avoid eventual discomfort, if not the chiropractor.

1 These leather supporters from the Fifties and Sixties display three variations on the western theme. Conchos in silver and brass, shown on the bottom belt, derived from early Hispanic cowpokes of the American southwest. ($75-125).

2 Two- and three-fingered leather mittens were lined with wool or sheepskin, with gauntlets to keep cold wind out of the sleeves. These were probably made in the Thirties. ($100-125).

3 More back/kidney belts of the Fifties show varying graphic renditions, including pouch pockets on the white ladies' model. ($75-125). The brown belt appears to be a home-made item, probably at a home in Iowa.

THE fact that belts served a rudimentary function was no reason for them to resemble prosthetic devices. Most motorcyclists of the Fifties and Sixties were a decorative bunch, and rarely missed the opportunity to adorn any surface with bangles and festive brightwork.

The primary artistic influences in the American idiom of art deco were the Native American artisans of the previous century. The tribes of the American southwest and Mexico, with strong Spanish influences, contributed the patterns and geometric designs widely adopted by 20th century motorcyclists, among others.

Despite the grim brutality administered the Native Americans by the U.S. military, the impact of their art survived to inform and inspire another generation of Americans. One outfit in Springfield, Massachusetts even named their motorcycle the Indian.

4 Belts of the Fifties and Sixties carried on the western motif, adding braided sections for some elasticity (beer storage). Riders often added their own decorations for personalized adornment. ($100-150).

5 Leather mittens with gauntlets offered another surface for costume jewelry. This pair displays a fine example of mid-20th Century American industrial folk art. ($100-125).

(All items courtesy of Wheels Through Time Museum, Mt. Vernon, Illinois).

N the Fifties, with the advent of Big Advertising, joined by Public Relations, Marketing and Publicity/Promotions, The Motor Company began expanding their line of legible clothing. More varieties and graphic representations of the company logo appeared on a wider range of clothing and accessories.

One engaging element of motorcycling has always been its novelty, an activity set distinctly apart from the motoring mainstream. And one aspect of the distinction was the willingness of its participants to dress funny.

1 The child's cotton bib was created in that period of confusion, circa 1954. when the company's actual birthdate was in doubt. Later 1903 was chosen as the inaugural year, enhancing the value of all the erroneous 50th anniversary items released in '54. ($80-120).

2 In the Sixties, illustrated T-shirts become a graphic arts industry, and billboards for patriotic sloganeering. ($5/20-30).

3 In the Seventies, Milwaukee covered fashions from formal to casual. This became a popular ensemble at Tennessee bachelor parties. ($8/25-75).

4 This polyester sport shirt from Richman Bothers has been traced to the mid-Seventies. According to rumor, a man named Kramer has offered $450 for this shirt. ($8/20-50).

(Items on this page courtesy of the Lu & Armando Magri collection).

NOVELTY doesn't necessarily require the costume of a clown, but the element of humor has played a leading role in the evolution of motorcycling attire.

As a graphic example, no one wearing the striped vest shown at the left is out to represent himself as person who takes himself too seriously. No, the vestments of the two-wheeled crowd are usually limited to proud displays of brand preference and/or the expression of fun and frolic associated with the sport.

But motorcycle clothing, at least outside of France, has never reached the *haute couture* level of fashion statement, and probably never will. This may well be inscribed as a Good Thing in the chronicles of father time. For there are those who have no need to know how much fun can be had while wearing leather clothes.

5 The Harley-Davidson bartender's vest is a prized garment at major barbecues, rallies, weddings, races, and any occasion when fine food and beverages are served. ($30-50). (Wheels Through Time Museum).

6 The ladies were not ignored by the marketing mavens in Milwaukee, as evidenced by this flowery thermal undershirt for her warm riding enjoyment. ($20-30). (Lu and Armando Magri collection).

7 In recent years H-D has expanded its line of formalwear with pictorial ties illustrating vintage machines and racing, American and fine art. Prices run from $14-17. (Dudley Perkins Company).

8 Milwaukee's most prominent logo of the early Seventies was the red-white-and-blue Number 1 symbol, created for the racing team. ($15-25). (Lu and Armando Magri collection).

METALWORK has always been the fundamental framework for motorcycle art and adornment. Iron and steel comprise the foundation of the motorcycle itself, so the representation of the sport in metal is a natural corollary.

Personal artifacts in steel, brass and pewter have been part of motorcycling from the beginning. After kidney belts, belt buckles were the next items in line to display the sentiments of both the fellow whose pants they held up, and the craftsmanship of those who etched tiny designs in metal. Belt buckles quickly became the most prominent, and functional, piece of costume jewelry in the world of motorcycling. Soon they passed from practical clothing cincher to collectible, and many were retired from pants duty.

1 A buckle miscellany from the Perkins collection. Enameled buckles were popular in the early Eighties; pewter renditions picture a flathead of the Thirties and a 1940 Knucklehead; two buckles mark the 80th anniversary of San Francisco's Dudley Perkins Company, and the large Harley-Davidson buckle portrays the Roaring Twenties. ($25-50).

2 These large pewter and brass buckles commemorate Harley-Davidson's 85th anniversary (3000 issued; $30/100), and the fiftieth Black Hills Motor Classic in Sturgis, South Dakota (5000 issued; $30/100). (Custom Chrome collection).

AS you can see here, some belt buckles were never even intended to hold up pants. The sequential series pictured in the case below was produced as a limited edition collector's item in 1986. The buckles illustrate, in fine detail, the development of Harley-Davidson engines from 1903 to 1984; a capsule history of the company in iron.

These buckles may never be reduced to the indignity of holding up trousers, but they will hold up in commercial value. Their market value has more than tripled in ten years, and will no doubt continue to rise.

3 The Motor Company's "Growth of a Sport" buckle, commemorating the first decade of production, 1994. ($55/75-100) (Dudley Perkins collection).

4 The 7-piece "Evolution of the V-Twin" set was issued in 1986. The sets included sequentially numbered buckles in a walnut frame. (5000 issued; $175/600). (Richard Callinan collection).

5 Top: This buckle recreates the cover of a 1919 H-D sales brochure (3000 issued; $60/75-150).
The large buckle commemorates 50th year of the OHV engine, 1989. (3000 issued; $60/200).
Bottom right: H-D 90th anniversary buckle, 1993. (3000 issued; $60/200). (Custom Chrome collection).

WHAT more can be said about the multi-faceted world of belt buckles? Except, perhaps, here are more belt buckles.

1 H-D 80th anniversary buckle, "Made in America" pictures the founding four, 1983. ($30/100-150).

2 H-D 75th anniversary buckle. 1978. ($12/225).

3 Solid brass Harley-Davidson of America buckle, 1981. ($14/25).

4 Oval eagle, 1980. ($30/40).

5 Live to Ride buckle, 1979. ($12/140).

6 V-twin bar & shield buckle, 1983. ($6/10).

7 Artisty in Iron show buckle, 1980 ($ unknown).

8 Official Low Rider buckle, 1980. ($7/20).

9 Police buckle, year and price unknown.

10 Number 1 logo, 1976. ($13/20).

11 The First Harley. ($13/25-40).

12 Eagle on bar and shield, 1985. ($16/25).

13 Sportster, 1977. ($7/40).

14 FLH 1200, 1978. ($7/40-50).

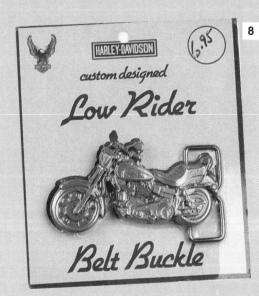

15

16

17

18

BUCKLES, buckles, buckles. These fasteners, none of which were produced as limited editions, have become collectible in spite of their common ancestry and absence of distinguished pedigree. They are just buckles.

But some of them do display a distinctive feature, heretofore unknown in the realm of fashionable clasps. Nude women with wings. The name of the artist who created these airborne beauties has been lost to history, but his work lives as a tribute to both flight and the female form. And as if that were not more than one might reasonably expect from a simple fastener, they still do a fine job of clamping on the pants.

19

20

These buckles were all issued in 1982 except for the eagle on black enamel at the lower right, which dates from 1977. None were produced as limited editions, but their values range from 50 percent higher to double or triple the original price.

15 Bar and shield with two nude, winged women. ($17/40).

16 Oval eagle head buckle. ($15/30).

17 Eagle bar and shield. ($15/30).

18 More winged women with bar and shield. ($16/50).

19 Eagle Made in USA buckle. ($15/30).

20 Eagle with Harley-Davidson script. ($17/30).

21 Oval winged woman rising. ($16/35).

22 Ebony eagle. ($11/20).

23 Eagle and bar shield. ($16/25-30).

(All buckles courtesy of the Lu and Armando Magri collection).

21

22

23

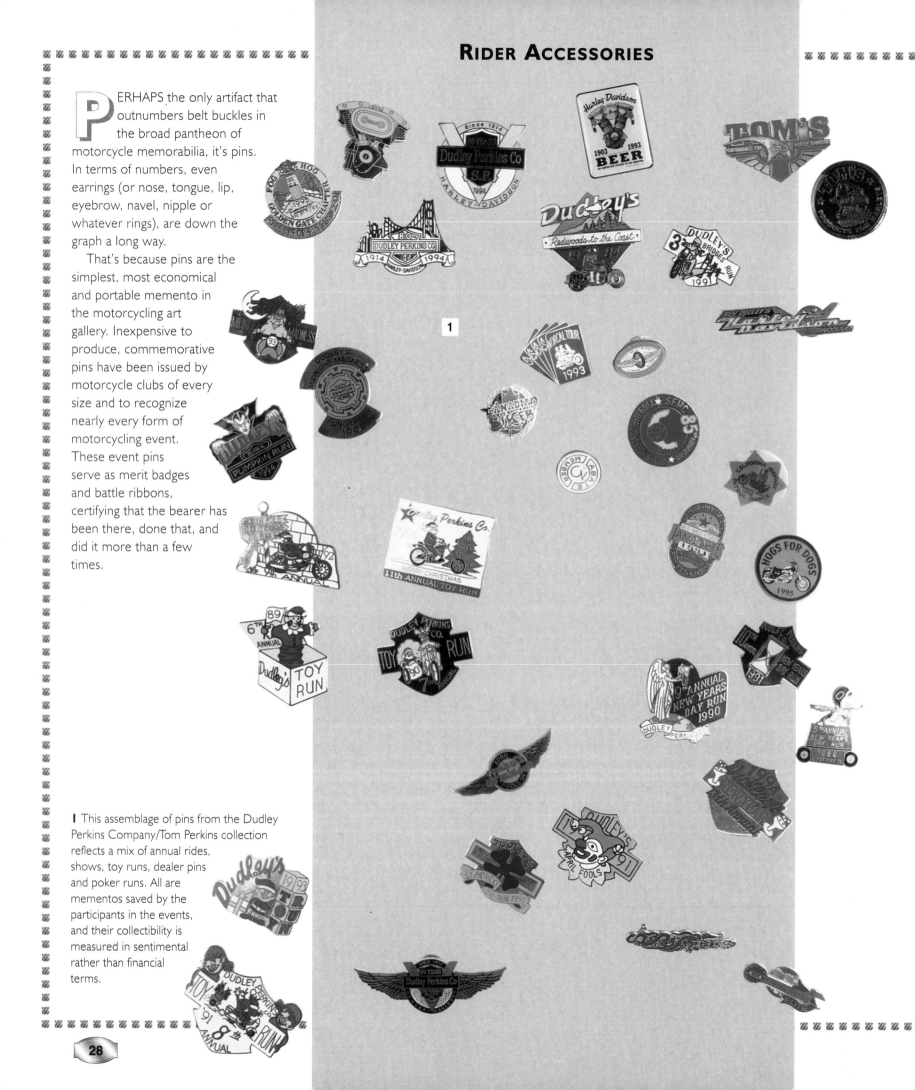

PERHAPS the only artifact that outnumbers belt buckles in the broad pantheon of motorcycle memorabilia, it's pins. In terms of numbers, even earrings (or nose, tongue, lip, eyebrow, navel, nipple or whatever rings), are down the graph a long way.

That's because pins are the simplest, most economical and portable memento in the motorcycling art gallery. Inexpensive to produce, commemorative pins have been issued by motorcycle clubs of every size and to recognize nearly every form of motorcycling event. These event pins serve as merit badges and battle ribbons, certifying that the bearer has been there, done that, and did it more than a few times.

1 This assemblage of pins from the Dudley Perkins Company/Tom Perkins collection reflects a mix of annual rides, shows, toy runs, dealer pins and poker runs. All are mementos saved by the participants in the events, and their collectibility is measured in sentimental rather than financial terms.

2 Here is another montage of miscellaneous pins from the same San Francisco collection. Included are some pins issued by Harley-Davidson, while others are dealer or special event pieces. Most of the Milwaukee renditions date from the mid-Seventies to mid-Eighties and sold for between $4 and $10. As a rule of thumb, most are now worth two to three times their original prices as collectibles.

(All items courtesy of Dudley Perkins Company/Tom Perkins collection).

1 Armando Magri was the Sacramento, California Harley dealer from 1950-1983. His framed pin collection, still displayed at the dealership, features AMA Gypsy tour pins and member pins and patches from 1931-1973. The market value of such a collection has little meaning for Magri, who would never sell it. But at auctions and swap meets such pins and awards generally sell for between $50 and $300.

2 A miscellany of promotional buttons (cheaper, oversized pins with a commercial sponsor) created from the Fifties through the Seventies. The button bearing the expression "When it snows we reign" refers to the Harley-Davidson snowmobile, produced from 1971-75. (Items 1-2 from the Lu and Armando Magri collection).

PINS, pins, pins. Another singular advantage for pin collectors is price, which stays consistently below most other forms of motorcycle memorabilia. Yet another benefit accrues from their size, since a considerable number can be stored in a fairly small treasure box, or worn on a jacket, vest or hat. Pins may be at the bottom of the economic scale in terms of collector value, but they serve as micro-memorials to the great rides and gatherings of a lifetime.

3 This medley of pins from the Sixties and Seventies originally sold for from $2-$8, and now bring from two to four times their purchase prices. The 75th Anniversary pin at the left has shown the most increase; originally priced at $4.50, it now sells for $20-$25. (Lu and Armando Magri collection).

4 The 1952 Harley-Davidson Dealers' Sales Conference button was once worn by Owen Aston of Parkersburg, West Virginia. ($25-300). (Richard Callinan collection).

5 The large Number I pin honored Scott Parker's second Grand National Championship in 1989; a limited edition of 1000. ($30-40).
The 90th Anniversary pin, produced in 1993, sold for $12 and now is priced from $20-25.
The early springer and WLA motorcycle pins date from the Eighties and sold for $4-6.
The winged bar and shield pin was made in 1980. ($3/10-15).
The 1957 Sportster pin was made in 1980. ($3/10-15). (Custom Chrome collection).

PATCHES generally don't achieve any significant status as collectibles in terms of price, since most were often produced in considerable numbers and sewn to jackets or vests. Period clothing from the Thirties through Fifties, still bearing original patches, may bring premium prices at auction, but most are usually handed down to family members and saved as personal mementos.

Of course hard times can force the sale of family memorabilia, when the choice between mementos and food on the table becomes simpler. But the purchase of other people's memories can be a difficult proposition, except in cases where the original owner was a celebrity. One recent example was the auction of the personal belongings of Jacqueline Kennedy, who probably never rode a Harley-Davidson.

1 This patchwork of patches displays a framework of Harley-Davidson logos employing the bar and shield, eagles, wings, flames and a prime number. The large numeral, in terms of collector value, ranks first. ($10-50). (The Shop collection).

2 The Harley Owners Group (HOG) issues anniversary patches. The California Highway Patrol patch is not intended for civilian application, and can lead to disputes with the authorities if worn improperly. ($ unknown). (Bob Kovacs collection).

EMBROIDERED patches, many of them quite stylishly rendered, have long been a standard motorcycle insignia. Here again, low cost is a factor, and many patches outlast the garments to which they are originally affixed, and get transfered to new clothing.

The Harley Owners Group, established in 1983, provides patches as part of the membership package. Most members wear them on their regular riding or touring gear, arranged either in annual succesion or mixed with other event patches and pins. Patches serve both as trophies and memories, ready to wear.

3 The two Northern California Tour patches fly above the sticker marking the 50th anniversary of the Harley-Davidson Club of Prague. The sticker turned up at a shopping center swap meet; thus the expression, the Czech is in the mall. ($ unknown). (Lu and Armando Magri collection)

4 This patch from the 1953 race in Dodge City, Kansas, sold originally for $1.00 and is now valued at $25-75. The traditional event was shadowed by the death of popular racer Billy Huber. (Pat and Al Doerman collection).

5 More HOG patches and a patch issued by the National Motorcycle Museum and Hall of Fame in Sturgis, South Dakota. ($ np). (Dudley Perkins collection).

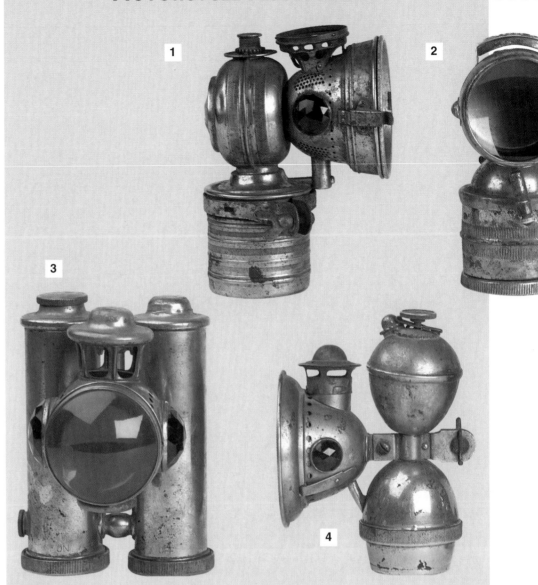

ILLUMINATION, or lack thereof, was the primary limitation on night riding in the early days, following dogs, rutted roads and horses. Electric lighting did become an option for motorcyclists in the late Teens, but early examples of co-generation were not noted for their reliability. Acetylene lamps at least lost their illuminating power gradually, rather than just plunging the rider into immediate darkness. Most motorcyclists chose gas lights until electrics became more trustworthy in the Twenties. With improved generators, batteries and bulbs, motorcycles moved into the modern age of American transportation.

1 A lamp made by the 20th Century Manufacturing Co, USA. ($100-150).

2 A Bauer headlamp made in Germany. ($100-150).

3 The Duplex lamp was made by Miller Daniels & Walsh of New York City in 1899. ($100-150).

4 The B&R Acetylene unit was patented in March 1899. ($100-150).

5 The SearchLight, made in the USA. ($200-250).

6 Improved Banner P&A light, made in the USA. ($200-250).

7 A Bett's Patent Headlight (patented June 4, 1895, by the 20th Century Manufacturing Company). ($200-250).

EARLY candlepower was provided by gas, which was created by dissolving carbide pellets in water. The water container usually served also as the perch for the lamp, and the whole assembly simply clamped to the handebar. The acetylene lamps did little to illuminate the roadway at anything above walking speed, but did provide a margin of safety by making the motorcyclist more visible to pedestrians and oncoming traffic.

As lamps and lenses increased in size so did the tanks, creating the need to mount the units separately and connect them by hose or tubing. Harley-Davidson contracted with several manufactuers of both gas and electric systems. The first model to roll out of Milwaukee with a factory-equipped headlight was the 11J twin in 1915. By 1920 Harley had developed their own electrical system.

8 The Perfection headlamp, USA, was patented March 20, 1899. It is shown here in front and side views. ($75-125).

9 Another 20th Century Manufacturing Company headlamp. ($100-125).

10 A light labeled The Liberty Model. ($100-125).

11 The Hine-Watt Columbia Automatic Gas Lamp with its original box and instruction booklet. It was patented by the Chicago company on October 10, 1899. ($3.10/150-200).

(All lamps courtesy of Wheels Through Time Museum, Mt. Vernon, Illinois).

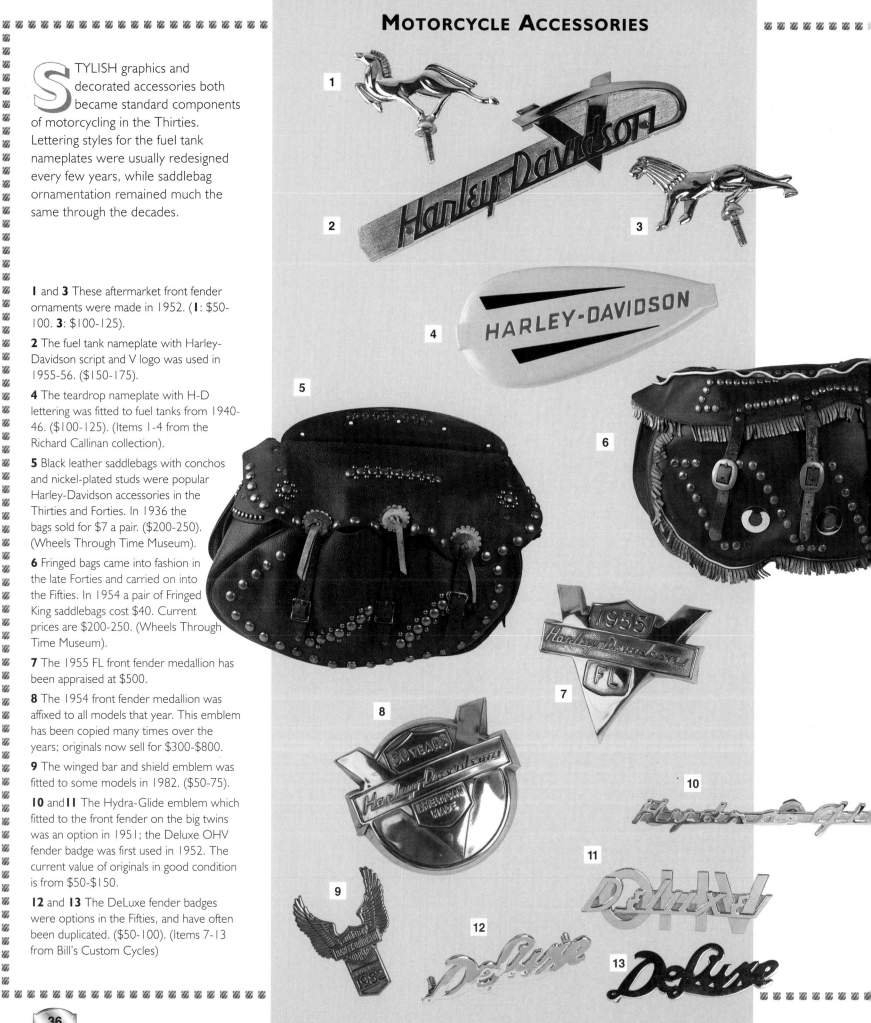

STYLISH graphics and decorated accessories both became standard components of motorcycling in the Thirties. Lettering styles for the fuel tank nameplates were usually redesigned every few years, while saddlebag ornamentation remained much the same through the decades.

1 and **3** These aftermarket front fender ornaments were made in 1952. (**1**: $50-100. **3**: $100-125).

2 The fuel tank nameplate with Harley-Davidson script and V logo was used in 1955-56. ($150-175).

4 The teardrop nameplate with H-D lettering was fitted to fuel tanks from 1940-46. ($100-125). (Items 1-4 from the Richard Callinan collection).

5 Black leather saddlebags with conchos and nickel-plated studs were popular Harley-Davidson accessories in the Thirties and Forties. In 1936 the bags sold for $7 a pair. ($200-250). (Wheels Through Time Museum).

6 Fringed bags came into fashion in the late Forties and carried on into the Fifties. In 1954 a pair of Fringed King saddlebags cost $40. Current prices are $200-250. (Wheels Through Time Museum).

7 The 1955 FL front fender medallion has been appraised at $500.

8 The 1954 front fender medallion was affixed to all models that year. This emblem has been copied many times over the years; originals now sell for $300-$800.

9 The winged bar and shield emblem was fitted to some models in 1982. ($50-75).

10 and **11** The Hydra-Glide emblem which fitted to the front fender on the big twins was an option in 1951; the Deluxe OHV fender badge was first used in 1952. The current value of originals in good condition is from $50-$150.

12 and **13** The DeLuxe fender badges were options in the Fifties, and have often been duplicated. ($50-100). (Items 7-13 from Bill's Custom Cycles)

14

15

16

17

18 AMF Harley-Davidson

19 HARLEY-DAVIDSON

20

21 HARLEY-DAVIDSON

22

THE Art Deco influence on graphic design had faded by the Forties, and company badges reflected more subdued styling cues. But the use of streamlined shapes survived, reflecting the images of speed and daring that symbolized the spirit of motorcycling. Following World War II the designs entered another period of revision, as America turned to yet more conservative fashions and a new framework of social responsibility.

More recently, the filigree and furbelows of the Thirties have come back on that round-trip train of fashion. And the pinstriping styles of the Fifties are also modern all over again.

14 The uppermost nameplate was a one-year-only badge on the Sportster fuel tank in 1961. ($200-300).

15 This circular logo was fitted to fuel tanks in 1957-58. ($200-300). (Items 14-15 from Bill's Custom Cycles).

16 The Harley-Davidson script appeared on the tanks from 1951-54. ($40-60).

17 Nameplate used from 1963-65. ($40-60).

18 The new AMF/Harley-Davidson logo first appeared on fuel tanks in 1972. ($40-60).

19 The shooting star emblem was the tank nameplate for 1961-62. ($40-60).

20 The arrow-bearing oval insignia was used in 1959-60. ($40-60).

21 The 1940-46 fuel tank nameplate. ($40-60). (Items 16-21 from The Shop collection).

22 This is a contemporary rendition of the traditional fringed leather saddlebag. ($40-60). (Wheels Through Time Museum).

TRENDS in graphic design are reflected by Harley-Davidson's changing advertising art and product labels through the decades. The most durable and consistent symbol in the Milwaukee lexicon has been the bar and shield emblem. The simplified block lettering appeared with the AMF merger in the late Sixties.

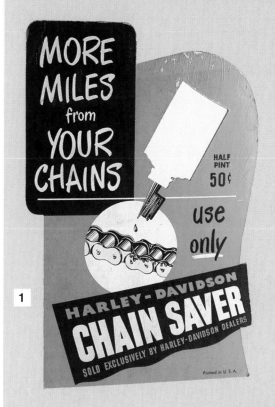

1 A Harley-Davidson Chain Saver counter display, circa 1950. ($75-150). (Wheels Through Time Museum).

2–4 These containers from the Forties include motor oil ($100), Gunk cleaner ($75) and silver engine paint ($25).

5–6 Two cans of oil from the Seventies. Pre-luxe was recommended for the big twins, and Premium Grade for Sportsters. ($25).

7 A can of 40weight two-stroke oil from the Sixties. ($20). (Items 2-7 from the Pat and Al Doerman collection).

8 Harley-Davidson aerosol spray paints from the Sixties, including sparkling burgundy and hi-fi purple blue and green. The cans include quick-drying enamel in jet fire orange and white and heat-resistant silver engine paint. ($25). (Mark George collection)

9–13 Paints and lubricants of the Seventies include **9** White spray enamel ($20), **10** Sunburst orange acrylic ($20), **11** Power Blend multi-grade oil ($40), **12** Premium Grade detergent oil ($40) and **13** Two-stroke oil ($40). (Items 9-13 from the Custom Chrome collection).

ORIGINAL, unopened Harley-Davidson oil cans have shown steady growth as collectibles. Age and condition figure most prominently in the value of these containers, with those from the pre-Teen era commanding the highest prices. The orange and black cans from the Twenties and Thirties rank next on the scale, with the rectangular and cylindrical 5-gallon cans the most highly valued.

Some of these cans have been repainted in the original colors, which is usually obvious when there is marked disparity between the old and new surfaces. A repainted can is generally valued some 30 to 40 percent lower than a container wearing its original paint.

14 A two-stroke oil can from the Forties ($50). (Pat and Al Doerman collection).

15 A Pre-Luxe oil counter display with responsible, helmet-wearing rider. ($125-150).

16 Harley-Davidson 5-gallon oil can from the Thirties, patented May 10, 1927 by the St. Louis Can Company. ($2000-2500).

17 The rectangular 5-gallon oil can from 1928 ($3000-3500).

18 Custom made combination passenger footrest and oil can carrier ($ np). (Items 15-18 from Wheels Through Time Museum).

19 A cross-section of lubricants from various eras including transmission oil, racing oil, Gunk degreaser, Hydra-Glide fork oil and chain grease. ($20-50). (Mark George collection).

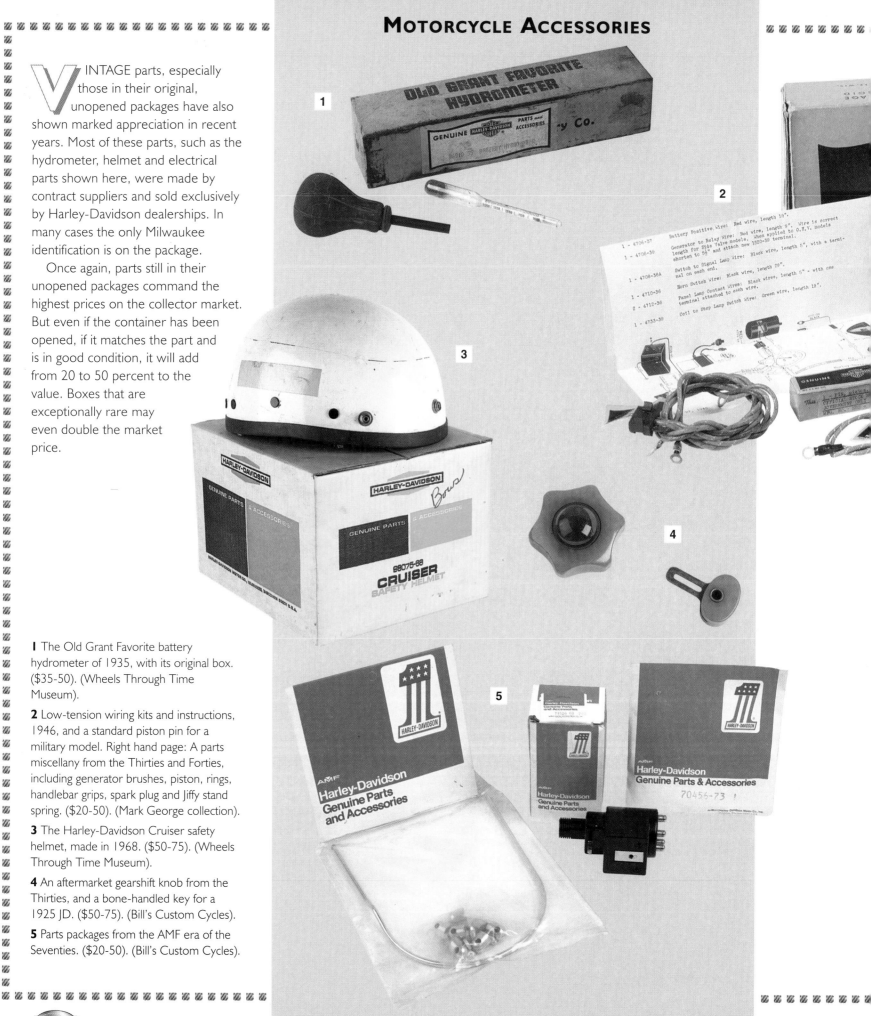

VINTAGE parts, especially those in their original, unopened packages have also shown marked appreciation in recent years. Most of these parts, such as the hydrometer, helmet and electrical parts shown here, were made by contract suppliers and sold exclusively by Harley-Davidson dealerships. In many cases the only Milwaukee identification is on the package.

Once again, parts still in their unopened packages command the highest prices on the collector market. But even if the container has been opened, if it matches the part and is in good condition, it will add from 20 to 50 percent to the value. Boxes that are exceptionally rare may even double the market price.

1 The Old Grant Favorite battery hydrometer of 1935, with its original box. ($35-50). (Wheels Through Time Museum).

2 Low-tension wiring kits and instructions, 1946, and a standard piston pin for a military model. Right hand page: A parts miscellany from the Thirties and Forties, including generator brushes, piston, rings, handlebar grips, spark plug and Jiffy stand spring. ($20-50). (Mark George collection).

3 The Harley-Davidson Cruiser safety helmet, made in 1968. ($50-75). (Wheels Through Time Museum).

4 An aftermarket gearshift knob from the Thirties, and a bone-handled key for a 1925 JD. ($50-75). (Bill's Custom Cycles).

5 Parts packages from the AMF era of the Seventies. ($20-50). (Bill's Custom Cycles).

PARTS AND ACCESSORIES

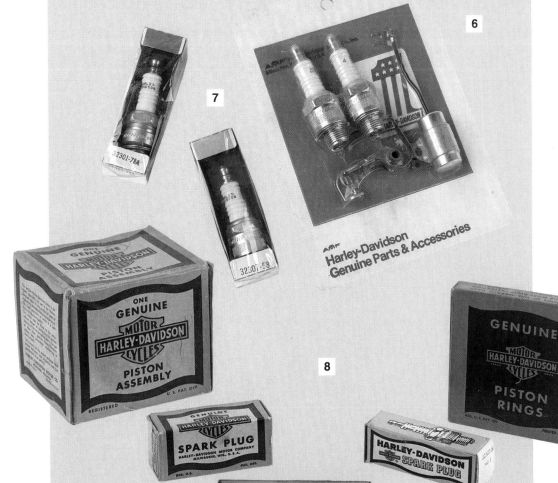

ORIGINAL factory replacement parts are referred to as new old stock (NOS), to distinguish them from later replacement or remanufactured parts. One reason for the rising prices of parts is the growing popularity of authentically restored motorcycles. Machines refurbished with NOS parts rate more highly than those fitted with aftermarket replacement pieces. So the competition between collectors and restorers has driven up the prices for original parts and accessories. All of which has been complicated by the growing production of counterfeit parts masquerading as NOS items.

So if someone is new to the collecting hobby, how is he or she to determine what is authentic and what is not? Ask an expert, and hope that he is qualified to make the distinction. Even in the fine arts, great forgeries often pass as the real things.

6 A 1977 AMF/Harley-Davidson tune-up kit with sparkplugs, points and condensor. ($15-20)

7 Spark plugs of 1958 and 1978. ($5-10).

8 Harley-Davidson replacement parts, left to right: piston assembly, 1952; spark plug, 1948; piston pin, 1932; spark plug, 1958; piston rings, 1940. ($15-20). (Items 6-8 from the Custom Chrome collection).

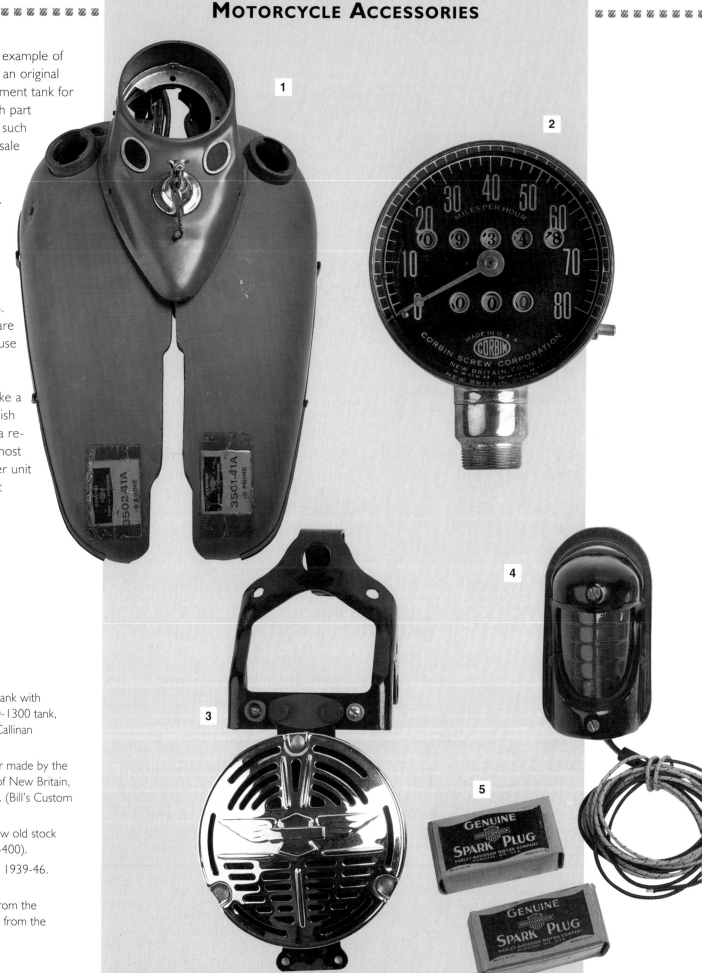

HERE is a prime example of new old stock, an original factory replacement tank for a 1941 Knucklehead, with part numbers attached. Many such parts were sold in wholesale lots when numerous dealerships went out of business in the Seventies. Others were purchased for restoration projects that never materialized, and many have been sitting on the same dusty shelves for over 50 years.

New old stock horns are widely sought after, because most originals eventually weathered and lost their finish. Of course it will take a discerning eye to distinguish between an original and a re-chromed piece. But for most restorers, if it's the proper unit for the model year, and it works, that is sufficient authenticity.

1 New old stock 1941 fuel tank with 1943-46 dash cover. ($1000-1300 tank, $175-225 cover). (Richard Callinan collection).

2 Early Thirties speedometer made by the Corbin Screw Corporation of New Britain, Connecticut. ($15/200-300). (Bill's Custom Cycles).

3 This horn assembly is a new old stock part from the Forties. ($300-400).

4 Beehive taillamp assembly, 1939-46. ($250-300).

5 Boxed spark plugs dating from the Forties. ($50-60). (Items 3-5 from the Richard Callinan collection).

SPEEDOMETERS have recently evolved into established collectibles, largely because they are assembled instruments. Speedos have moving parts – shafts, gears and stuff – and also display the graphic styles of their era in numbers and letters. As functional instruments showing speed and distance, they are mechanical and artistic representations of motorcycle form and function, pieces of time. And they are neat to look at.

Items such as the E-Z-C (get it?) memo holder below show an even more basic recording device. This item was popular with delivery services, postal and police departments.

6 Rare 1953 counter-clockwise speedometer adapted for racing at Daytona Beach. The big twin instrument was reconfigured for the K model, which had reverse cable gearing. The standard K speedometer (shown below) was too small to read at racing speeds. ($800).

7 Speedometer for 1952 K model made by Stewart-Warner. ($100-200). (Items 6-7 from Bill's Custom Cycles).

8 Big twin air cleaner cover, 1946 ($350-400).

9 Handlebar grips of the same era. ($100-125).

10 The E-Z-C memo pad holder, with built-in pencil holder, attached to the handlebar. A product of the Thirties, the clipboard was popular with police and delivery riders. ($150-250). (Items 8-10 from the Richard Callinan collection).

FLAGS, banners and pennants have figured strongly in Harley-Davidson advertising efforts since the earliest publicity efforts originated in Milwaukee. Football and baseball had made pennants a favored form of public support from fans, and since motorcycling was touted as "The Greatest Sport of All," flying your own brand was a natural counterpart. These pennants were in virtually continuous production from the late Teens through the Fifties, with surprisingly little change in style.

Nylon banners, such as the one shown celebrating Harley-Davidson's 50th anniversary, were usually dealer items which automatically meant limited editions. Others were produced for major racing meets, rallies, trade shows and annual dealers' meetings.

1 Harley-Davidson 50th Anniversary nylon banner, valued at $250-500.

2-4 AMA official tour patches from the Forties and Fifties, $30-100. (Items 1-4 from Wheels Through Time Museum).

5-6 Official factory pennants of the Fifties, $50-150. (Richard Callinan collection).

7 Collage of Fifties' pennants with H-D eagle medallion, made by Lu Magri. Value approximately $1500. (Lu and Armando Magri collection).

8

MORE intricate artwork was usually reserved for banners celebrating major landmarks in Harley-Davidson's history, in this case the 75th Anniversary. This linen wall hanging traces the development of Milwaukee production from the backyard shed in 1903 through the anniversary Sportster and Electra-Glide models in 1978. In between are the highlights from each era in the company's first three-quarters of a century; the functional motorcycle truck of 1915, the World War I military model, the famous single cylinder Peashooter racer, and the legendary Knucklehead of 1936.

The pictograph also marks the beginning of the modern era in roadracing and dirt track, Milwaukee's long-standing involvement in police motorcycles, and the longest-running model in the company roster, the 3-wheeled Servi-Car. Graphic works depicting the upcoming 100th anniversary will likely show an even greater range of detail.

8 The 75th anniversary banner, 1978, illustrating the development of Harley-Davidson models over the years. The linen wall hanging is currently valued at $50-75. (Pat and Al Doerman collection).

MANY collectors prize the early owners' manuals, rider handbooks, repair bulletins and sales brochures. The prices have not reached astronomical figures yet, since so many of these early texts and documents have been kept in excellent condition over the decades. And because they were produced in relatively large numbers, compared to other types of printed memorabilia.

But here again, the value is enhanced by the competition between collectors and restorers, or owners of vintage Harleys who seek the correct manuals for their machines.

Age and condition are again the uppermost considerations in pricing these items.

1 and 2 Open is the Harley-Davidson Rider's Handbook for 1924. The yellow-cover booklet is the 1935 handbook for the 45 Twin. In good condition, these booklets have current market values from $50-150. (Wheels Through Time Museum).

3 Rider Handbook for the Topper, Harley-Davidson's motor scooter, 1964. ($20-30).

4 Electra-Glide Rider Handbook for 1965. ($20-30).

5 The 1958 Rider Handbook for the 165cc two-stroke. ($10-20).

6 Electra-Glide Rider Handbook for 1967. ($15-20).

7 Rider Handbook for the 1966 XLCH Sportster. ($20-30). (Items 3-7 from the Mark George collection).

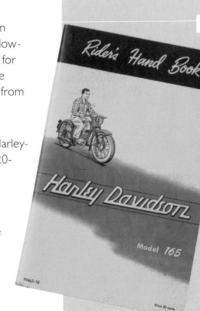

SOME of the most highly valued documentation of Harley-Davidson history are those documents which never left the original dealership. Such is the case with the 1915 sales catalog shown here, which has probably remained in the files at San Francisco's Dudley Perkins Company for the last 82 years.

The same is true for many of the later owner's manuals, which were kept in stock for customers who lost their originals or subsequent owners of the motorcycles who didn't receive a manual with the purchase.

8 Original Harley-Davidson sales catalog for 1915. Current value, $150-$400. (Tom Perkins collection).

9 Servi-Car Rider Handbook. ($30-40).

10 1962 Rider Handbook covers the Pacer, Scat and Ranger two-strokes. ($20-30).

11 1964 Rider Handbook for the FL Duo-Glide. ($40-50).

12 1964 Rider Handbook for the XL Sportster. ($40-50).

13 Servi-Car handbook. ($20-30).

14 Electra-Glide Rider Handbook for 1965. ($40-50). (Items 9-14 from the Mark George collection).

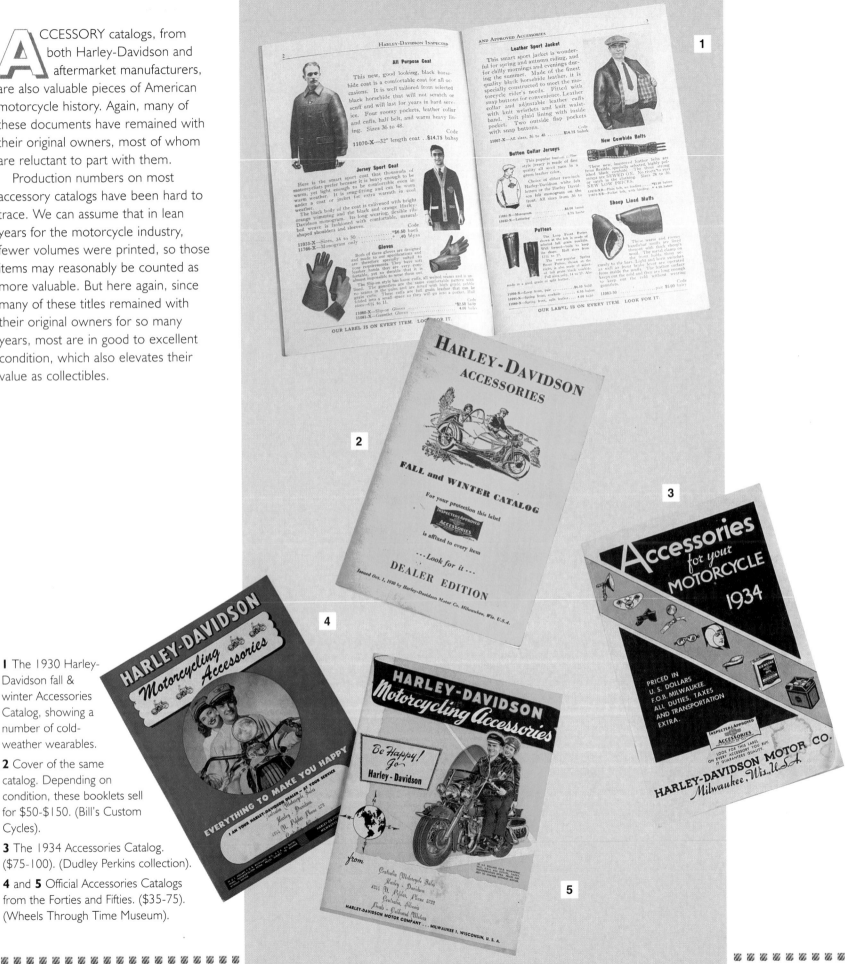

ACCESSORY catalogs, from both Harley-Davidson and aftermarket manufacturers, are also valuable pieces of American motorcycle history. Again, many of these documents have remained with their original owners, most of whom are reluctant to part with them.

Production numbers on most accessory catalogs have been hard to trace. We can assume that in lean years for the motorcycle industry, fewer volumes were printed, so those items may reasonably be counted as more valuable. But here again, since many of these titles remained with their original owners for so many years, most are in good to excellent condition, which also elevates their value as collectibles.

1 The 1930 Harley-Davidson fall & winter Accessories Catalog, showing a number of cold-weather wearables.

2 Cover of the same catalog. Depending on condition, these booklets sell for $50-$150. (Bill's Custom Cycles).

3 The 1934 Accessories Catalog. ($75-100). (Dudley Perkins collection).

4 and **5** Official Accessories Catalogs from the Forties and Fifties. ($35-75). (Wheels Through Time Museum).

IKE most collectible items, earlier examples of factory-produced booklets are highest on the price scale. Condition often becomes a secondary consideration when the material is genuinely antique and very few examples remain. Some motorcyclists have been surprised at how early the aftermarket accessory business developed. The example shown on this page dates from 1916, and apparently had then reached its 13th year of publication. Note the banner headline; "We prepay all orders amounting to 50 cents or more," referring to shipping charges.

6 Accessories Catalog from 1947. ($35-75).

7 Early Fifties Accessories Catalogs. ($35-75).

8 The 1954 Accessories Catalog. ($35-75). (Items 6-8 from Wheels Through Time Museum).

9 This booklet entitled "Let's visit the Harley-Davidson Factory" was published in 1936. Its current value is in the region of $75-100. (Dudley Perkins collection).

10 Aftermarket accessories and equipment catalogs appeared early on in American motorcycling history. The 1916 Motorcycle Equipment Company's Guaranteed Motorcycle Supplies catalog was the 13th annual edition.

11 Cover of the 1915 edition of the Guaranteed Motorcycle Supplies catalog, published by the Motorcycle Equipment Company of Hammondsport, New York. Catalogs such as these often sell for $75-250. (Items 10 and 11 from Bill's Custom Cycles).

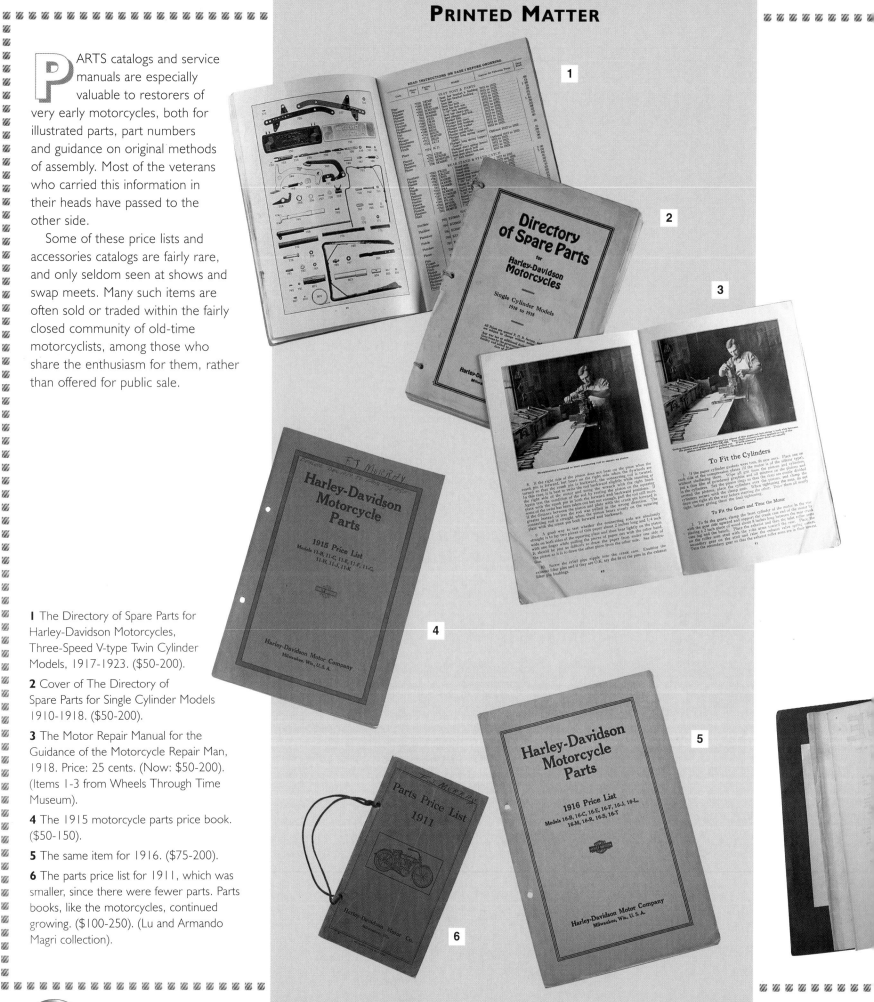

PARTS catalogs and service manuals are especially valuable to restorers of very early motorcycles, both for illustrated parts, part numbers and guidance on original methods of assembly. Most of the veterans who carried this information in their heads have passed to the other side.

Some of these price lists and accessories catalogs are fairly rare, and only seldom seen at shows and swap meets. Many such items are often sold or traded within the fairly closed community of old-time motorcyclists, among those who share the enthusiasm for them, rather than offered for public sale.

1 The Directory of Spare Parts for Harley-Davidson Motorcycles, Three-Speed V-type Twin Cylinder Models, 1917-1923. ($50-200).

2 Cover of The Directory of Spare Parts for Single Cylinder Models 1910-1918. ($50-200).

3 The Motor Repair Manual for the Guidance of the Motorcycle Repair Man, 1918. Price: 25 cents. (Now: $50-200). (Items 1-3 from Wheels Through Time Museum).

4 The 1915 motorcycle parts price book. ($50-150).

5 The same item for 1916. ($75-200).

6 The parts price list for 1911, which was smaller, since there were fewer parts. Parts books, like the motorcycles, continued growing. ($100-250). (Lu and Armando Magri collection).

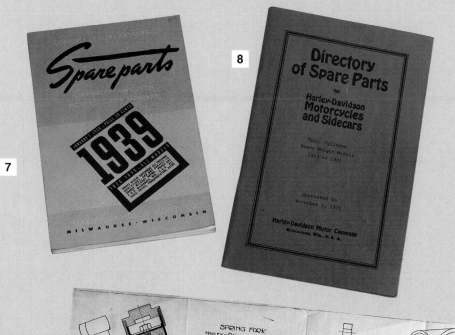

7

8

9

THIS page may well contain the single most valuable Harley-Davidson document in this or any other book. It is a full-scale engineering drawing for the first Harley spring fork, designed and drawn by William S. Harley. The date is 1907.

7 The 1939 dealer's catalog of spare parts, covering all models from 1926-1939. ($100-150). (Lu and Armando Magri collection).

8 Spare parts directory for big twins from 1913-1921. ($150-200). (Dudley Perkins Collection).

9 This document may justly lay claim to being unique; that is, one of one. By all appearances, it is the original engineering drawing for the Harley-Davidson spring fork, drawn to full scale by William S. Harley, and dated November 18, 1907. Drafted on heavy vellum, the drawing measures 19 inches x 27 inches, and is in remarkably good condition. When asked about the probable dollar value of this drawing, Magri said, "I have no idea what it's worth. But I don't want to sell it." (Lu and Armando Magri collection).

10 Bound copies of the original Shop Dope service manuals of the Thirties; the open page shows details of the 1935 Forty-five transmission with reverse, used in the Servi Car. ($200-300). (Wheels Through Time Museum).

11 The 1954 parts index for competition motorcycles. ($50-100). (Bill's Custom Cycles).

10

11

NATURALLY the factories and aftermarket manufacturers had no exclusive on the production of printed matter. Magazines and books on motorcycling appeared quickly and in increasing numbers with the growth of the sport.

1 Ralph Victor's "Boy Scouts Motor Cycles" came out in 1911. ($40-75).

2 "Motorcycle Chums in the Land of the Sky," by Andrew Carey Lincoln was one of a popular series, and was published in 1914. ($40-75).

3 "Boy Scouts on Motorcycles or With the Flying Squadron" appeared in 1912. ($40-75).

4 "Bert Wilson's Twin Cylinder Racer," by J.W. Duffield, was published in 1914. ($40-75).

5 Ralph Marlow's "The Big Five Motorcycle Boys At The Front," also part of a series, appeared in 1915. ($40-75).

6 The cover of the March 1947 Motorcyclist shows the Daytona Beach starting line. ($0.20/15-30). (Items 1-6 from Wheels Through Time Museum).

7 Official Harley-Davidson bookends, 1996. ($78). The books within them are "Harley-Davidson – The Ultimate Machine," by Tod Rafferty, Running Press, 1994 ($30/50). "American Racer 1940-1980," by Stephen Wright, Motorbooks International, 1989 ($40/50).

8 The Literary Digest for November 3, 1917. The cover illustration, entitled "The Dispatch Bearer," shows a Harley rider in action during World War I. ($0.10/30-50). (Dudley Perkins collection).

MAGAZINE coverage of motorcyling has been extensive since the earliest days of the sport. *Motorcycle Illustrated* debuted in 1906 and ran ads on the cover. Periodicals were the prime source for specifications on new machines, racing coverage, club news, editorial commentary and advertising from the manufacturers.

Within a few years *Motorcycle & Bicycle Illustrated* was on the market, as were *Western Bicyclist & Motorcyclist* and *Motorcycling*.

9–11 *Motorcycling* magazine was published in Chicago; these 1912 issues show a club run on one cover, a 2-page Harley-Davidson ad, and an illustration of a motorcycle patrolman apparently threatening heavyweight boxing champion Jack Johnson with a terminal parking citation. ($.10/75-100).

12–13 Two copies of the American Motorcycle Association magazine, The Motorcyclist, published in Los Angeles. In 1943 it became the AMA News, changed in 1947 to American Motorcycling, and later to its current title, American Motorcyclist. ($15-20). (Items 9-13 from Wheels Through Time Museum).

14 The first and only edition of the *Harley Rider* comic book, 1988 by Carl Hungness Publishing. ($2/25). (Tom Brannan collection).

15–17 Three copies of American Motorcycling from the Fifties. The left and right issues are from 1951; the March 1957 edition at center pictures James Stewart as Charles Lindbergh in the film "Spirit of St. Louis." The famed aviator was an avid motorcyclist. ($0.25/15-20). (Wheels Through Time Museum).

THE Harley-Davidson *Enthusiast* magazine was first published in 1916, and is still issued regularly from Milwaukee. In February 1938 the title was shortened to simply *The Enthusiast*.

Over the years the magazine has chronicled the development and shifting fortunes of The Harley-Davidson Motor Company. After decades as a monthly, *The Enthusiast* shifted to bimonthly publication in the Seventies and later was changed to a quarterly which it remains today. Circulation for the most recent quarter (1996) was over a half-million.

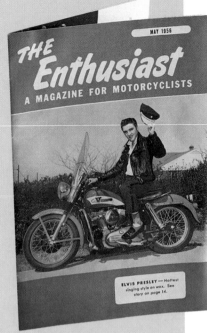

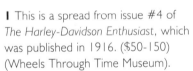

1 This is a spread from issue #4 of *The Harley-Davidson Enthusiast*, which was published in 1916. ($50-150) (Wheels Through Time Museum).

2 One of the most highly valued copies of *The Enthusiast* is the May 1956 issue featuring the young rockabilly star Elvis Presley on a Model K on the cover. The photo of the King has increased the price to $75-250. (Bill's Custom Cycles).

3 This montage indicates the varieties of graphic styles used on the magazine's cover before and after World War II. For a period in the Fifties and Sixties, the title was changed to *the motorcycle ENTHUSIAST in action*, for some reason. (Thirties, $20-60); (Fifties, $10-30). (Wheels Through Time Museum).

HERE is another selection displaying issues of *The Enthusiast* from the Thirties, Forties and Fifties. The British collection of magazines at the top of the page includes the subscriber's mailing envelope from 1951, when postage was inexpensive.

4 The August 1951 issue featured a club rally in Michigan. ($10-50).

5 The photo-illustration cover from September 1957 heralded the new Duo-Glide. ($10-50).

6 The November 1946 issue showed a Harley-Davidson on peacetime courier duty. ($10-50).

7 A bold rider aviates the K model on the April 1953 cover. ($10-50).

8 In December 1942, *The Enthusiast* marked the first anniversary of U.S. involvement in World War II with a feature on U.S. Army Signal Corps dispatch riders. ($10-50).

9 Paul Goldsmith takes the checkered flag at Daytona on the cover of the April 1953 edition. ($10-50).

10 For September 1953 *The Enthusiast* featured Harley-Davidson's fiftieth anniversary. ($10-50). (Items 4-10 from the Mark George collection).

11 and **12** Leatherette bound copies of *The Enthusiast* from 1941 and 1937. The rider with the helmet, about to take over second place, is Armando Magri. ($300-400). (Lu and Armando Magri collection).

PHOTOGRAPHY was well established as a prominent medium for news, features and advertising by the time motorcycles came along. Harley-Davidson was among the pioneers in photographic ads, using both original and retouched pictures in their catalogs, posters and magazine layouts.

Most of the location and studio photography covering Harley's first half-century was done by Pohlman Studios of Milwaukee. Many of the photos that were not used for ads or in *The Enthusiast* were never identified or cataloged at the time. Only in the last few years has the Harley-Davidson Archives been able to determine some of the names and dates for early photos, and to catalog and file them.

1 This reprint of a 1911 photograph displays Milwaukee's early involvement with the U.S. Post Office, which used Harley-Davidson machines for rural mail delivery. ($35-50). (Custom Chrome collection).

2 This attractive and stylishly dressed young woman is astride a 1937 Harley-Davidson 45 Twin, and is obviously ready to ride. ($ np). (Dudley Perkins collection).

3 This 1988 reprint of a factory advertising photo from 1923 shows William Davidson, in the sidecar, and William Harley. Though the photograph was intended to promote the sporting versatility of the Harley-Davidson 1200cc JD model and Royal Tourist sidecar, the suits and ties were more than a little out of character. Of the founding four, only William Davidson chose not to ride motorcycles. ($30/35-50). (Custom Chrome collection).

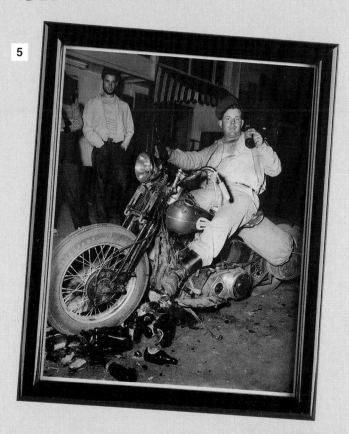

PROBABLY the most famous Harley-Davidson photo in history (5) is the one that Milwaukee would have most liked to see destroyed.

4 The 1930 fleet of California Highway Patrol bikes lined up for delivery in front of Frank J. Murray's Harley-Davidson dealership in Sacramento. ($ np). (Lu and Armando Magri collection).

5 The famous "outlaw biker" photograph. This picture of an unidentified party animal was taken in Hollister, California on July 4, 1947, by news photographer Barney Petersen. The Boozefighters Motorcycle Club and other high-spirited motorcyclists were on hand for the annual races and revelry, which led to some tomfoolery in the streets of the small California town. The activities were described by the media as a riot, adding that many of the townsfolk feared for their lives.

To make a short story legend, the incident formed the basis of Stanley Kramer's 1953 film "The Wild One," starring Marlon Brando and Lee Marvin. In the American tradition of transposing cause and effect, the film would be blamed for motorcycling's "image problem." ($35-75). (Dudley Perkins collection).

6 Dudley Perkins seems quite pleased to be surrounded by a troupe of young ladies in jumpers bearing the curious lettering, M-G-M STUDOIS, and wearing hats from The May Company department store. ($ np). (Dudley Perkins collection).

POSTERS naturally played a significant role in Harley-Davidson's advertising and promotion campaigns, which were orchestrated by Arthur Davidson. Color illustrations generally ranked higher than photography in the advertising art of the Twenties and Thirties, and were regarded as a touch of class in the marketing of all products.

1 This poster was created to celebrate the 80th anniversary of the Dudley Perkins Company of San Francisco. The Harley-Davidson dealership opened in 1914 and has remained under family ownership ever since. Artist: Michael Hinton. ($ np). (Dudley Perkins collection).

2 Much of the early advertising art aimed to persuade customers that the sidecar-equipped motorcycle was a reasonable alternative to the automobile. And that it was far more economical. ($100-200). (Dudley Perkins collection).

3 Special sale sign from the Fifties emphasizes low down-payment and easy terms. ($100-150). (Pat and Al Doerman collection).

4 One of the most widely reproduced Harley posters features the sporting rider of 1928. This print was taken from an original by the Smithsonian Institution in Washington, D.C. in 1986. Auction prices for original posters range from three to twelve thousand dollars. (Dudley Perkins collection).

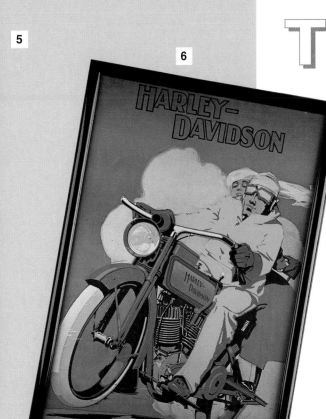

THE art of the motorcycle has grabbed the imaginations of designers, illustrators, sculptors, graphic artists and stylists ever since the first machines hit the road. The bikes offer a broad range of bits and pieces where the eye can linger, and riders add the dynamic imagery of action and fun on wheels.

5 Harley-Davidson managed to combine traditional design elements with the Peter Max style to create this bicentennial poster in 1976. The company produced special Liberty Edition versions of the Super Glide and FLH models, embellished with graphics in the style shown on the poster. ($25-75). (Lu and Armando Magri collection).

6 This advertising poster, produced in 1916, portrays the excitement, fun and fashion of two-wheeled transportation. This is one of the first wheelie illustrations used to dramatize the sporting flavor of motorcycling. Note the passenger's sidesaddle position. Artist: H.I. Piggelen. ($250-400) (Dudley Perkins collection).

7 One of a series of Harley prints by Art One Images of Monterey Park, California, 1990. The '58 Panhead was illustrated by Jack Knight. This photo-realistic style has gained considerable popularity in recent years.($50-75). (Harley-Davidson of Sacramento).

"SPEED that leaves autos behind in the dust!" Advertising and sales literature has never lacked for superlatives or enthusiasm. Magazine ads often pulled extra duty as flyers and sales brochures.

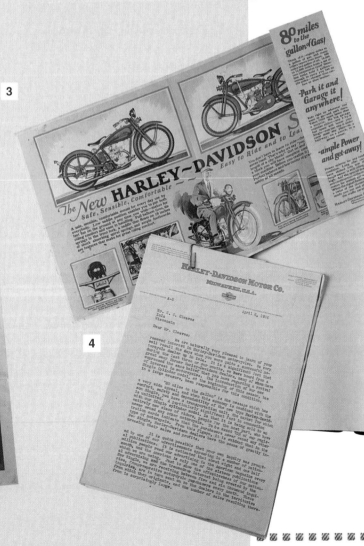

1 This is a reprint of a 1929 sales flyer and it includes all the appeals and benefits for the new motorcycle owner. KP Company, 1977. ($5-10). (Lu and Armando Magri collection).

2 Harley-Davidson still markets its early advertising art in the form of these embossed tin reproductions of hand-tinted photographs from the Twenties. H-D, 1995. ($18). (Dudley Perkins collection).

3 This 1914 advertising layout is a good example of Harley-Davidson's early emphasis on basic engineering principles and strong components. The vast majority of motorcyclists had a mechanical bent, were interested in how things worked, and learned to make most of their own repairs. ($50-150).

4 In 1926 the push was on to promote the Model B, Harley's first vertical single-cylinder machine in eight years. The 500cc single was offered in both flathead and overhead valve models, plus a racing version. The advertising campaign is explained in the accompanying letter to Mr. Cleaves. (Brochures, $25-50). (Items 3-4 from Wheels Through Time Museum).

5

5 This embossed metal sign replicates another hand-tinted advertising layout from the Thirties. The Package Truck was touted as a practical delivery vehicle for the small business, and offered better economy than a four-wheeled truck. This ad illustrates a number of applications for the commercial side-wheeler. H-D, 1994. ($18). (Dudley Perkins collection).

6 This print from 1920 is another version of Harley-Davidson's concerted effort to promote sidecar rigs as both practical and sporting transportation. Already the industrial behemoth loomed on the American landscape, and the appeals of fishing, camping and hunting became forceful motivations. ($200-250). (Custom Chrome collection).

7 These are original printer's blocks for Harley-Davidson advertisements in the Twenties, reversed here to show how they would have printed. From the left: an F model of the Teens; the J model with sidecar, circa 1922; sign art for a bike/sidecar plan proclaiming just $2.50 down-payment; magazine ad for the 1929 single with "5 Big New Features." ($50-150). (Pat and Al Doerman collection).

6

7

MAGAZINE advertising has become increasingly popular as a collectible, and has remained fairly affordable because there is so much of it remaining in good condition. Harley-Davidson advertised consistently since its inception, and invested heavily in print ads even during periods when the market was in decline.

1 This fold-out brochure was reprinted from an ad in the November 1947 issue of *American Motorcycling*. This layout includes the entire Milwaukee lineup, with technical details on the new Panhead engine. ($100-150). (Wheels Through Time Museum).

2 This 1938 ad shows two happy riders on the 1000cc Knucklehead, which was offered in red, blue, green or tan. Half the layout is devoted to more utilitarian aspects of motorcycling. ($65).

3 Ads from the August and September 1949 issues of The Enthusiast. This was the first year for the new Hydra-Glide front fork. ($50-100). (Items 2-3 from the Custom Chrome collection).

4 This spiral-bound booklet featured the Harley-Davidson model lineup for 1939. Shown is the 750cc WL model, which sold for $355. ($300-400). (Wheels Through Time Museum).

THE avenues for advertising expanded in the Thirties, as the company and its dealers sought new ways to entice customers during the lean years of the Great Depression.

5 The 1938 calendar from Schaber's Cycle Shop of Ithaca, New York indicates a genuine full-service dealership, including lawn mowers, tricycles and baby carriages. Calendars were and are steadfast forms of dealer advertising. ($30-75). (Mark George collection).

6 This home-made collage employs the cover of the 1940 Harley-Davidson sales brochure as a centerpiece. ($ np). (Wheels Through Time Museum).

7 This poster features a cutaway drawing illustrating the inner workings of the 1948 Panhead engine. Most of these posters deteriorated after long periods on the motorcycle shop walls, but those that were stashed away are now valuable. ($50-350). (Wheels Through Time Museum).

8 Direct mail advertising gained strength in the Thirties, and astute dealers sent postcards to their customers. Space at left was reserved for dealer's imprint. ($25-50). (Mark George collection).

9 The cover of a fold-out brochure featuring the new models for 1939. ($25-75). (Wheels Through Time Museum).

COMPETITION among motorcycle manufacturers heated up in the Fifties. With more builders entering the American market, advertising came to play an even more important role in the business.

1 This embossed metal sign reproduces a 1958 store poster heralding the arrival of the Duo-Glide, the first Harley-Davidson with rear suspension. Made in Great Britain. ($10-20). (Bob Kovacs collection).

2 This postcard from the Fifties features an illustration of the 165cc two-stroke, Harley-Davidson's entry in the lightweight market. ($5-10).

3 This dealer postcard is a colorized photo of two All-American youngsters riding a pair of 125cc two-strokes. ($5-10). (Items 2-3 from the Mark George collection).

4 Folding, triangular cardboard showroom display sign from 1963 that proclaims the advantages of the small Topper scooter. This was the year William G. Davidson, a founder's grandson, joined the company as styling director. ($100-125). (Wheels Through Time Museum).

5 This dealership postcard from the Fifties was used to bring customers in for the opening of the spring riding season. ($10-20). (Mark George collection).

6

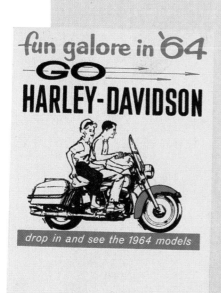

7

8

9

10

ALTHOUGH Arthur Davidson, last of the four founders, died in 1950, the advertising and promotion programs he originated remained in effect for many years.

6 Folding display card for the 1963 Pacer and Scat, which featured the first rear suspension for the lightweights. ($100-125).

7 A dealer display card with a motivational message designed to encourage early orders for the 1951 Panheads. The Hydra-Glide name, first used to designate the front fork in 1949, soon became the model name for the motorcycle itself. ($50-100). (Items 6-7 from Wheels Through Time Museum).

8 This illustrated 1954 postcard shows a casually-dressed young couple enjoying the scenery on a Hydra-Glide. ($5-10). (Mark George collection).

9 The magazine ad announcing the debut of the 1952 K model, surrounded by a throng of lilliputian admirers and flag-waving majorettes. The new 750cc flathead, with foot shift and hand clutch, was heavily promoted as a middleweight sporting twin, but the early models were underpowered. But the factory's tweaked racing versions did well, and led to the development of the Sportster five years later. ($20-30). (Dudley Perkins collection).

10 A dealer postcard urging customers to "drop in and see the 1964 models." The happy couple are riding an FL Duo-Glide. ($5-10). (Mark George collection).

SIGNS of the times: although graphic styles are always shifting, Milwaukee's marketing imagery has remained consistent over the decades. The bar and shield emblem, introduced in the Teens, remains the company's foremost logo. The other image most often associated with Harley-Davidson is the United States' national bird, the bald eagle. The majestic bird of prey has figured prominently in the company's advertising and promotion since the patriotic themes of the Seventies.

1 The eagle with bar and shield combination has been crafted in nearly every sort of material, including neon tubing. This example adorns a wall at Tramontin Harley-Davidson in New Jersey. ($4000). (Tramontin H-D).

2 The bar and shield proved to be an elastic symbol, easily stretched to emphasize the company name. This dealership sign was used for nearly four decades. ($150-200). (Wheels Through Time Museum).

3 Harley-Davidson was one among several companies who marketed Gunk degreaser under its own label. This billboard thermometer, circa 1952, was made by the Pam Clock Company of New Rochelle, New York. ($150-750). (Bill's Custom Cycles).

4 This pastoral scene is painted on wood siding, with a cast-resin motorcycle attached. The framed piece is 3 x 2 feet in size. Artist unknown. ($200/300-500). (Bob Kovacs collection).

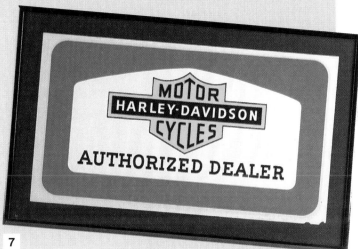

HARLEY-DAVIDSON effectively created a brand identity that came to achieve instant recognition around the world. The company has vigorously continued its efforts to maintain and protect that identity in all its national and international markets.

5 This is a cardboard dealership sign from the Twenties, when Harley-Davidsons were green and lovely young women wearing stylish hats rode in sidecars, and the motoring world was young. ($75-300). (Wheels Through Time Museum).

6 Metal Harley-Davidson Oil sign of the Forties, with chalk board. ($100-500). (Pat and Al Doerman collection).

7 This authorized dealer sign was issued by the factory in the Twenties. ($200-300).

8 This is a hand-painted rendering of the popular Smithsonian poster pictured earlier. The work was apparently commissioned by Harley-Davidson of Washington around 1953. Artist: F. Maré. ($10,000).

9 A metal authorized dealer sign, circa 1939, from the Tulsa Motorcycle Company of Oklahoma. ($600-700). (Items 7-9 from Wheels Through Time Museum).

HARLEY-DAVIDSON, under the marketing principles instituted by Arthur Davidson, maintained regular channels of communication with their dealers; this was one reason why the company could claim to have the strongest dealer network in the country, and eventually in the world.

1 This framed montage displays several of the marketing efforts for 1935. The letter is a direct appeal to the customer from Arthur Davidson himself, sent to riders in rural areas not served by a local dealership. The order blank was included to solicit orders direct from the factory. ($300-400).

2–5 The history of a sale: Albert Irvin bought his 1927 Harley-Davidson JD from Floyd Clymer in 1928. The original bill of sale shows a dealer price of $230; the retail price was $320. Motorcycle dealers owned a good profit margin in those days. Also shown are the owner's motorcycle license and registration. Judging by the varied addresses, Albert moved around some as worker for the Western Union Line Gang. ($100-150). (Items 1-5 from Wheels Through Time Museum).

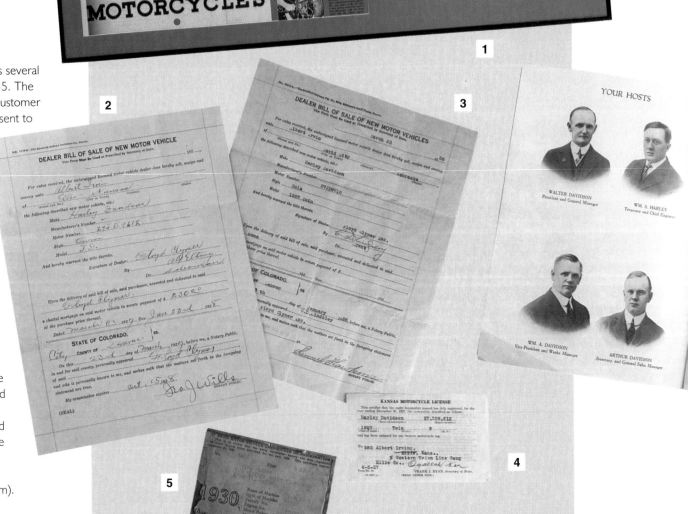

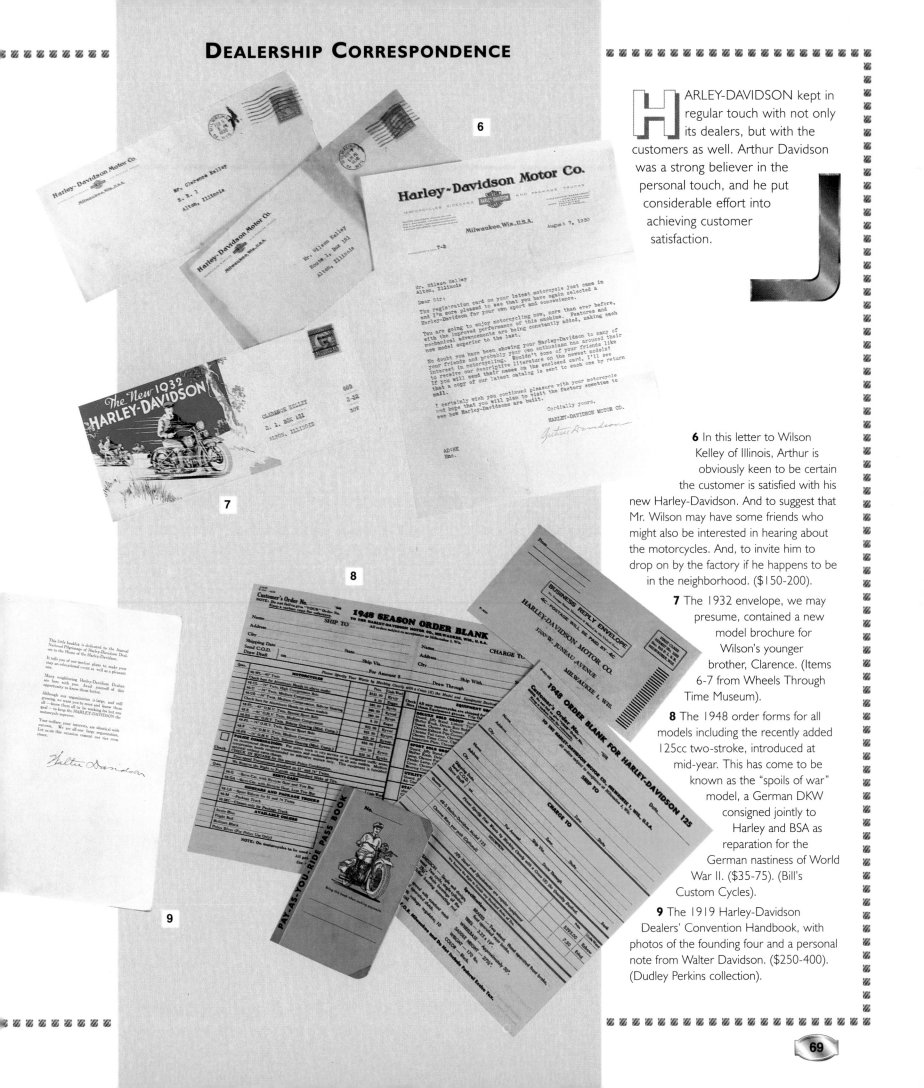

HARLEY-DAVIDSON kept in regular touch with not only its dealers, but with the customers as well. Arthur Davidson was a strong believer in the personal touch, and he put considerable effort into achieving customer satisfaction.

6 In this letter to Wilson Kelley of Illinois, Arthur is obviously keen to be certain the customer is satisfied with his new Harley-Davidson. And to suggest that Mr. Wilson may have some friends who might also be interested in hearing about the motorcycles. And, to invite him to drop on by the factory if he happens to be in the neighborhood. ($150-200).

7 The 1932 envelope, we may presume, contained a new model brochure for Wilson's younger brother, Clarence. (Items 6-7 from Wheels Through Time Museum).

8 The 1948 order forms for all models including the recently added 125cc two-stroke, introduced at mid-year. This has come to be known as the "spoils of war" model, a German DKW consigned jointly to Harley and BSA as reparation for the German nastiness of World War II. ($35-75). (Bill's Custom Cycles).

9 The 1919 Harley-Davidson Dealers' Convention Handbook, with photos of the founding four and a personal note from Walter Davidson. ($250-400). (Dudley Perkins collection).

N more recent years Harley-Davidson recognized the depth and commitment of the collector market, and began producing limited edition commemorative issues in various forms to appeal directly to it. From plaster to porcelain to pewter to stone, with steel, brass, silver and gold thrown in, Milwaukee commissions a panoramic landscape of arts and crafts every year.

1

1 The shadowbox sets of pewter miniatures commemorate milestone motorcycles in Harley's history. The Series 2 collection, "The Innovative Years," includes the streamlined 1925 JD, 1936 EL Knucklehead, 1942 XA military prototype, and the 48 FL Panhead, the last springer frame. Limited edition of 1000, 1987. ($290/750). (Richard Callinan collection).

2 Harley-Davidson's 85th anniversary in 1988 was marked with the production of two sets of medallions, one in gold plate and the other silver. The gold set was limited to 250 examples. ($600/700-800). (Dudley Perkins collection).

3 For their 90th year in business, Milwaukee minted a collection of 24 bronze ingots depicting an array of models spanning the decades. Limited edition # unknown, 1992. ($1500). (Wheels Through Time Museum).

2

3

4

PEWTER became the most prominent medium for Harley-Davidson collectibles, not least because of its affordability. Silver and gold editions naturally attract more affluent customers.

4 The Series 3 shadowbox collection, "The Legendary Years," includes the 1952 K model, 1961 Sportster XLCH, 1965 Electra Glide and 1971 Superglide. Limited edition of 1000, 1987. ($310/600-750). (Richard Callinan collection). The first shadowbox issue, "The Early Years," was produced in an edition of 5000 ($270/500-600) and the final set in the series, "An American Tradition," was made in 1988 in 1000 examples. ($350/600-750).

5 The 90th anniversary silver edition of ingots was struck in 1992 and produced as an edition of 12,000. The engraved ingots are .999 silver. ($500-750). (Dudley Perkins collection).

6 The silver series in the 85th Anniversary Collection. These medallions, cast in bronze then silver plated, were issued in a limited edition of 1000. 1987. ($480/550-650). (Richard Callinan collection).

5

6

SMALL (3-5 inches, 8-13cm wide) pewter figurines on a variety of motorcycling themes grew steadily in popularity in the late Eighties and early Nineties. The fact that they were offered in limited, numbered editions added to their desirability.

1 This pewter statuette is titled "On Patrol," and was issued in 1996 in a limited edition of 1500. ($70-80). (Custom Chrome collection).

2 This pewter figure of the reading rider was titled "Coffee Break." This was the first in a series of sculptures by Skip Winn and was produced in 1991. Limited edition, number unknown. ($55/300-400). (Bob Kovacs collection).

3 This 1992 pewter figurine, "Catch of the Day," was a limited edition of 2500. Artist: Skip Winn. ($60/250-350).

4 The wheeling racer on a Harley KR was produced by Skip Winn in 1994. Not a limited edition. ($58). (Items 3-4 from Tramontin Harley-Davidson).

5 Another Skip Winn figure in pewter, the vintage delivery rider and his pugnacious bulldog. It is titled "Trusty Friends" 1991. ($55/100). (Custom Chrome collection).

PEWTER MODELS

THE work of Skip Winn caught the fancy of the motorcycle public and led to a continuing series of figurines. Other artists joined the movement and the small pewter figures spread far and wide.

6 The highway patrolman and his trusty mount was issued in 1991. Artist: Skip Winn. ($55/100-150).

7 This figure is called "Rest Stop Be-Bop," another Skip Winn creation from 1993. ($55/100). (Items 6-7 from the Bob Kovacs collection).

8 This painted pewter figurine on a hardwood base features Mickey and Minnie Mouse. The statuette, titled "Two Wheeling," was a limited edition of 950 from MetalART USA. ($500/850). (Lu and Armando Magri collection).

9 "Continually Moving Towards the Future," issued in 1995 by Harley-Davidson as a limited edition of 1024, for dealers only. Artist: John A. Balistren. ($1500-2000). (Tramontin Harley-Davidson).

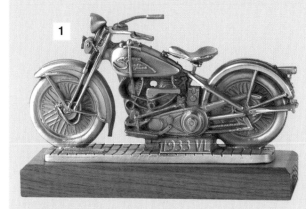

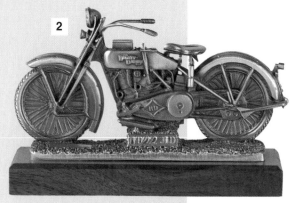

THE pewter models illustrated here, anchored securely to a walnut base, are desktop favorites among Harley-Davidson fans. The small sculptures, which are replicas of both antique and more recent milestone Harley-Davidson motorcycles, show up on bookshelves and dashboards as well.

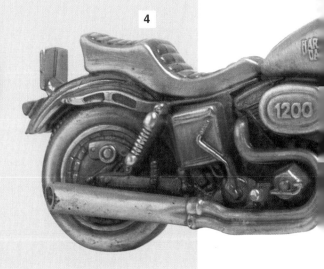

1 Pewter miniature: 1933 VL. Produced in 1993. Not a limited edition piece. ($55).

2 Pewter miniature: 1922 JD. Produced in 1993. Not a limited edition piece. ($55).

3 This 1991 FXSTC Softail Custom was offered in a limited edition of 3000 in 1991. ($40/500-600). (Items 1-3 from the Bob Kovacs collection).

4 This pewter 1977 Low Rider, though not made as a limited edition, is fairly rare and relatively valuable. 1988. ($40/300-400). (Richard Callinan collection).

5 The XLH Sportster was issued in 1994 in an edition of 7500. ($50-60). (Bob Kovacs collection).

6 This figure represents the 1936 EL speed record bike ridden by Joe Petrali at Daytona Beach. The record (136mph, 219km/h) was actually achieved with the aft bodywork removed. 1995. ($75-100). (Tramontin Harley-Davidson).

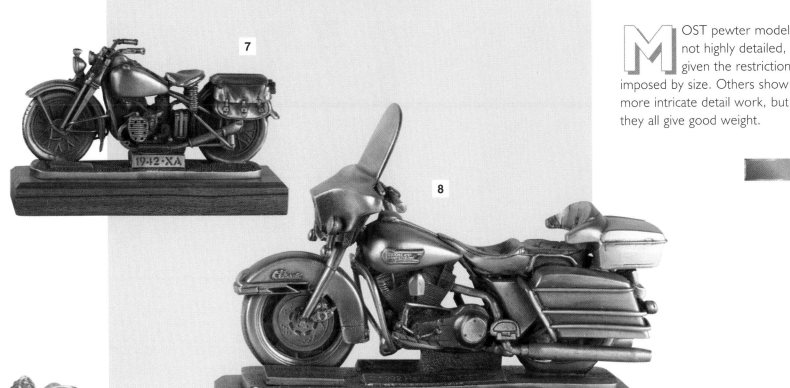

MOST pewter models are not highly detailed, given the restrictions imposed by size. Others show more intricate detail work, but they all give good weight.

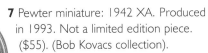

HARLEY-DAVIDSON
1918 EIGHT VALVE RACER ___ of 1000

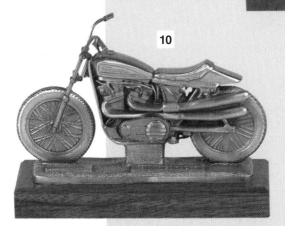

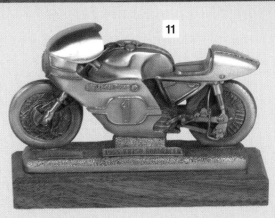

7 Pewter miniature: 1942 XA. Produced in 1993. Not a limited edition piece. ($55). (Bob Kovacs collection).

8 The sculpted FLHTC Electra Glide Classic was issued as a limited edition of 4000 in 1992. ($50/80-100). (Bob Kovacs collection).

9 This pewter rendition of the 1918 eight-valve racer is actually in larger scale than most of the figurines. The limited edition of 1000 was produced in 1987. ($250/400-500). (Custom Chrome collection).

10 This tribute to the legendary XR 750, based on the 1977 iteration, was issued in 1995. Not a limited edition. ($85).

11 The 1955 XR 750 factory roadracer shines with the luster of Daytona victories from years gone by. 1995, not a limited edition. ($55). (Items 10-11 from Tramontin Harley-Davidson).

THE marriage of motorcycling and pewter continued to expand into other forms, some functional and others purely decorative. Small, well-crafted, limited edition issues, such as many of these replicas are, have naturally proved very popular with Harley-Davidson devotees.

1–3 Official Harley-Davidson commemorative shot glasses in pewter, each in limited editions of 5000. From the left: "Growth of a Sport," 1996; "Roaring into the Twenties," 1994; "Growing Stronger Through Hard Times," 1995. ($35-38/75-125).

4 and **5** These commemorative engine models were issued in editions of 10,000. Shown here are the Knucklehead, 1936-47, (1996), and the Panhead, 1948-64, (1994). ($48).

6 and **7** The use of pewter for commemorative issues eventually extended to plates, with scenes engraved in bas relief. "The Birth of a Legend," with a scene from the early 1900s, was a limited edition of 3000. 1991 ($120/145). "The Spring Races," depicting an early racing scene at Daytona Beach, was issued in a limited edition of 1500. 1991. ($100/200-250). (Items 1-7 from Tramontin Harley-Davidson).

8

9

10

11

SOMETHING of the mechanical essence of motorcyles is transmitted in the medium of combined tin, brass, copper and lead. The forms seem to naturally follow the function.

8 and **9** "Roaring into the Twenties" expands the sidecar-with-flapper scene shown on one of the shot glasses. This pewter commemorative plate was produced in a limited editon of 3000. 1994. ($130/150-175).
"Growing Stronger Through Hard Times" honors the WPA workers of the Thirties. A limited edition of 3000. 1995. ($130/150-175).

10 The pewter version of the Shovelhead engine, 1966-84, was issued in 1995 in an edition of 10,000. ($48). (Items 8-10 from Tramontin Harley-Davidson).

11 The four-piece "Legends" set by sculptor Mark Patrick displays the motor history in pewter on a walnut base. From the left: Knucklehead, Panhead, Shovelhead and Evolution engines. The series was produced in 1991 as a limited edition. ($350-400). (Custom Chrome collection).

LEGENDS
By Mark Patrick

VINTAGE guns and knives are popular commemorative artifacts among Harley-Davidson enthusiasts, reflecting the pioneer spirit of American independence and rugged individualism. The first knife, an Aurum folding unit, was issued in 1979 in an edition of 3000.

1 This black powder pistol marked the 75th anniversary of the first Harley-Davidson V-twin in 1984. The pistol set, with case, powder flask and ramrod, was produced in a limited editon of 1000. ($400/500-600). (Richard Callinan collection).

2 The return to private ownership in 1981 was commemorated with a Gerber knife in a limited editon of 3000. The handles were each separately carved from Cordia hardwood. The 5.25-inch (13.3cm) blade, made of surgical stainless steel, is etched on both sides. ($150/$1000-1300). (Lu and Armando Magri collection).

3 The Buck Geronimo V-Twin knife replicates Geronimo's dagger, with the 1936 Knucklehead and 1986 Evolution engines in 22-carat gold overlay. The ground stag handle has nickel silver guard and butt. ($200/700-800). (Richard Callinan collection).

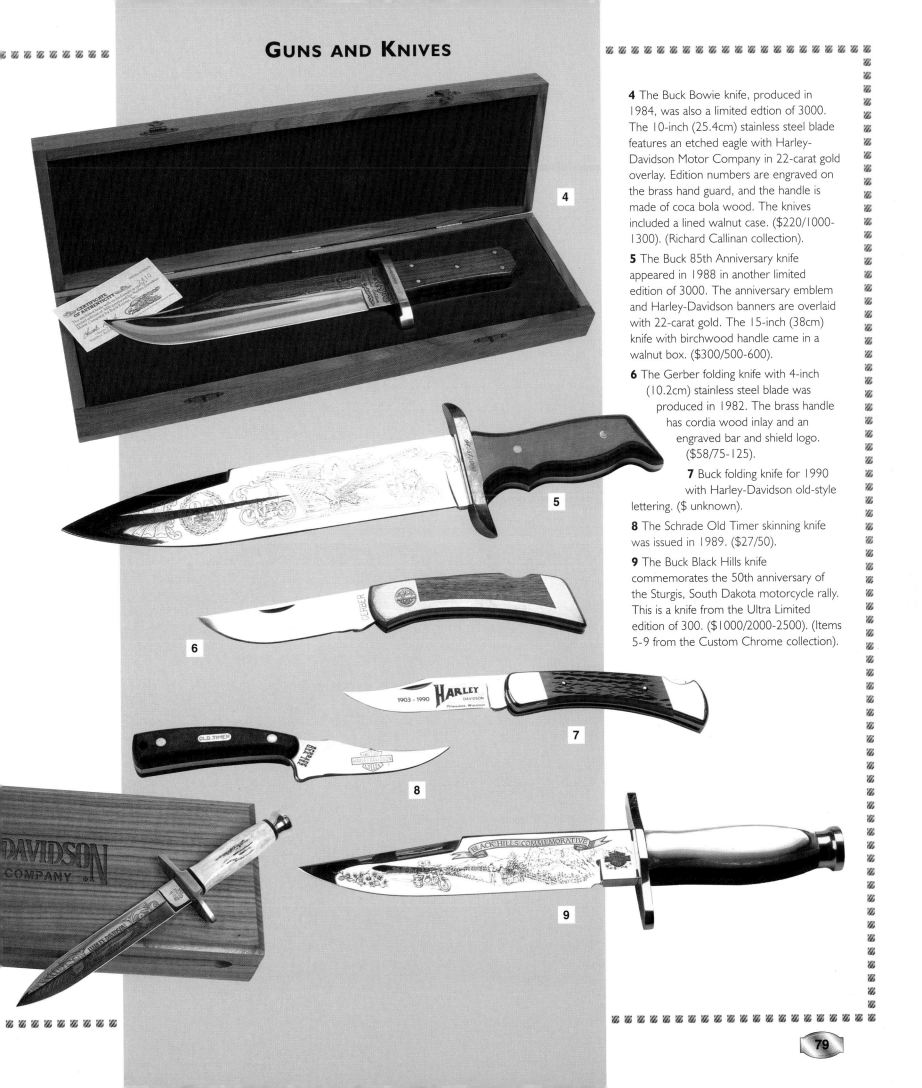

4 The Buck Bowie knife, produced in 1984, was also a limited edtion of 3000. The 10-inch (25.4cm) stainless steel blade features an etched eagle with Harley-Davidson Motor Company in 22-carat gold overlay. Edition numbers are engraved on the brass hand guard, and the handle is made of coca bola wood. The knives included a lined walnut case. ($220/1000-1300). (Richard Callinan collection).

5 The Buck 85th Anniversary knife appeared in 1988 in another limited edition of 3000. The anniversary emblem and Harley-Davidson banners are overlaid with 22-carat gold. The 15-inch (38cm) knife with birchwood handle came in a walnut box. ($300/500-600).

6 The Gerber folding knife with 4-inch (10.2cm) stainless steel blade was produced in 1982. The brass handle has cordia wood inlay and an engraved bar and shield logo. ($58/75-125).

7 Buck folding knife for 1990 with Harley-Davidson old-style lettering. ($ unknown).

8 The Schrade Old Timer skinning knife was issued in 1989. ($27/50).

9 The Buck Black Hills knife commemorates the 50th anniversary of the Sturgis, South Dakota motorcycle rally. This is a knife from the Ultra Limited edition of 300. ($1000/2000-2500). (Items 5-9 from the Custom Chrome collection).

THE knives displayed on these two pages show some of the finely crafted detail applied to the instruments, as well as the rare materials employed in their manufacture. The pink ivory wood used in the handle of knife (1), scientific name *Rhamnus zeyheri*, is extremely rare. The tree is a protected species in Africa. The mammoth ivory in the handle of the same knife is about 2000 years old.

1 The 90th anniversary dagger by Gerber measures 13.5 inches (34.3cm) overall, with a blade of high carbon steel. The eagle with bar and shield and U.S.A. emblem is etched in gold and silver on a deep blued chrome finish. The guard and butt cap are solid yellow brass with white brass and black fiber spacers. The handle is pink ivory, the royal wood of the Zulus, which grows only on the African plains. Heavier than oak or walnut, the pink wood turns brown with exposure to sunlight. The inlaid oval of mammoth ivory on the handle features individually etched scrimshaw illustrations. 1992. (Edition of 3000, plain handle, $500-600). (Edition of 500. $4000-5000).

2 The Buck Live To Ride knife was an Ultra Limited edition of 300 issued in 1992. ($700/1250-1400).

3 The Buck Black Hills knife commemorates the 50th anniversary of the Sturgis, South Dakota rally. The blade features a rally scene with 22-carat gold overlay banner. Compare this knife with item (9) featured on page 79. Limited edition of 3000, 1990. ($300/450-600). (Items 1-3 from Tramontin Harley-Davidson).

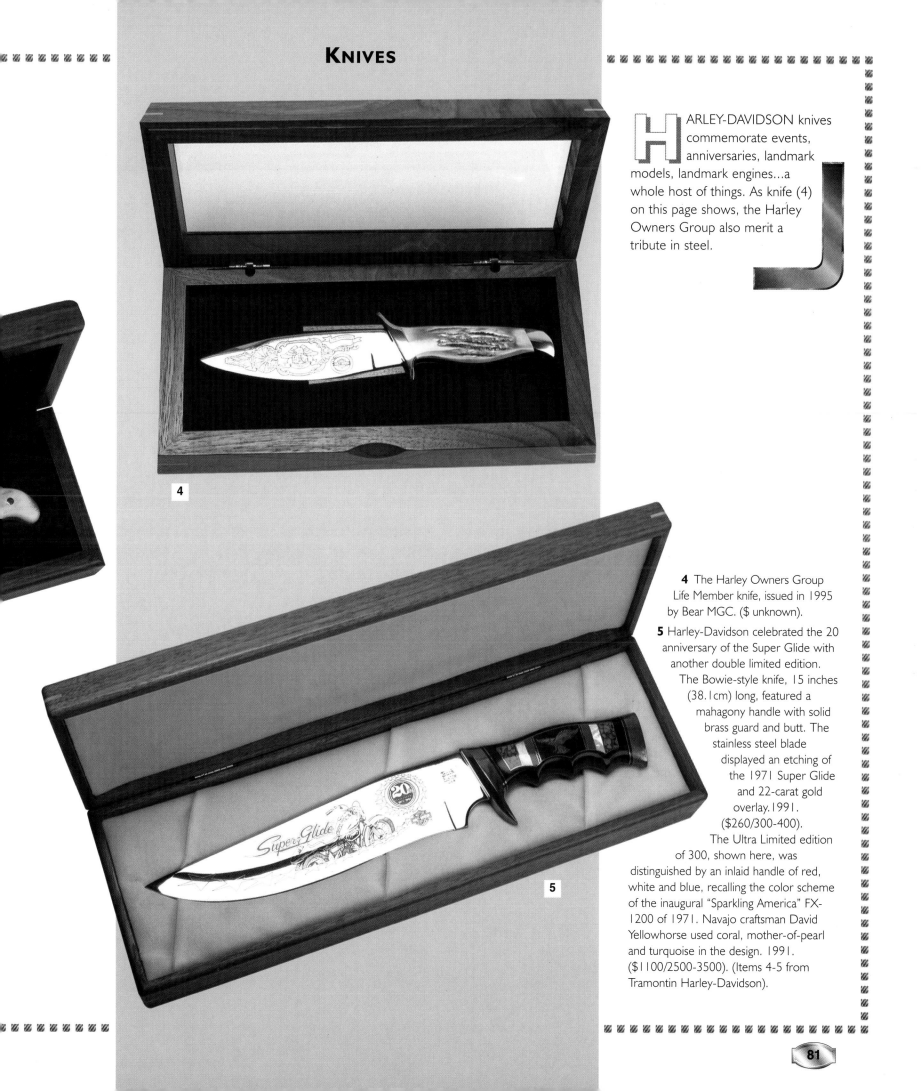

HARLEY-DAVIDSON knives commemorate events, anniversaries, landmark models, landmark engines...a whole host of things. As knife (4) on this page shows, the Harley Owners Group also merit a tribute in steel.

4 The Harley Owners Group Life Member knife, issued in 1995 by Bear MGC. ($ unknown).

5 Harley-Davidson celebrated the 20 anniversary of the Super Glide with another double limited edition. The Bowie-style knife, 15 inches (38.1cm) long, featured a mahagony handle with solid brass guard and butt. The stainless steel blade displayed an etching of the 1971 Super Glide and 22-carat gold overlay.1991. ($260/300-400).

The Ultra Limited edition of 300, shown here, was distinguished by an inlaid handle of red, white and blue, recalling the color scheme of the inaugural "Sparkling America" FX-1200 of 1971. Navajo craftsman David Yellowhorse used coral, mother-of-pearl and turquoise in the design. 1991. ($1100/2500-3500). (Items 4-5 from Tramontin Harley-Davidson).

As you may well imagine, none of these knives is used for hunting, fishing, whittling, or paint removal. These are art knives.

1 and **2** Editions One and Two of the Buck V-Twin Series, featuring the Flathead (top) and the Knucklehead models. Both, issued in limited editions of 3000, featured etched illustrations of the motorcycles and engines with 22-carat gold overlay. ($235/300-350). The Ultra Limited edition of 500, shown here, have inlaid handles finished in turquoise and gold. 1994. ($400-500).

3 Number seven in a series of ten Heritage Edition Buck folding knives salutes the Club Ride, 1948. Limited edition of 3000. 1996. ($150/175). (Items 1-3 from the Custom Chrome collection).

4 Number four in the Heritage Series, Country Roads, 1919. Limited edition of 3000. 1993. ($145/170-200). (Dudley Perkins collection).

5 and **6** The second and third Heritage Edition folding knives by Buck. From Humble Beginnings depicts the original factory of 1903. Limited edition of 3000. 1991. ($110/250-300). The Early Racers, with bone white handle, shows a 1917 dirt track race. Limited edition of 3000. 1992. ($135/200-250). (Custom Chrome collection).

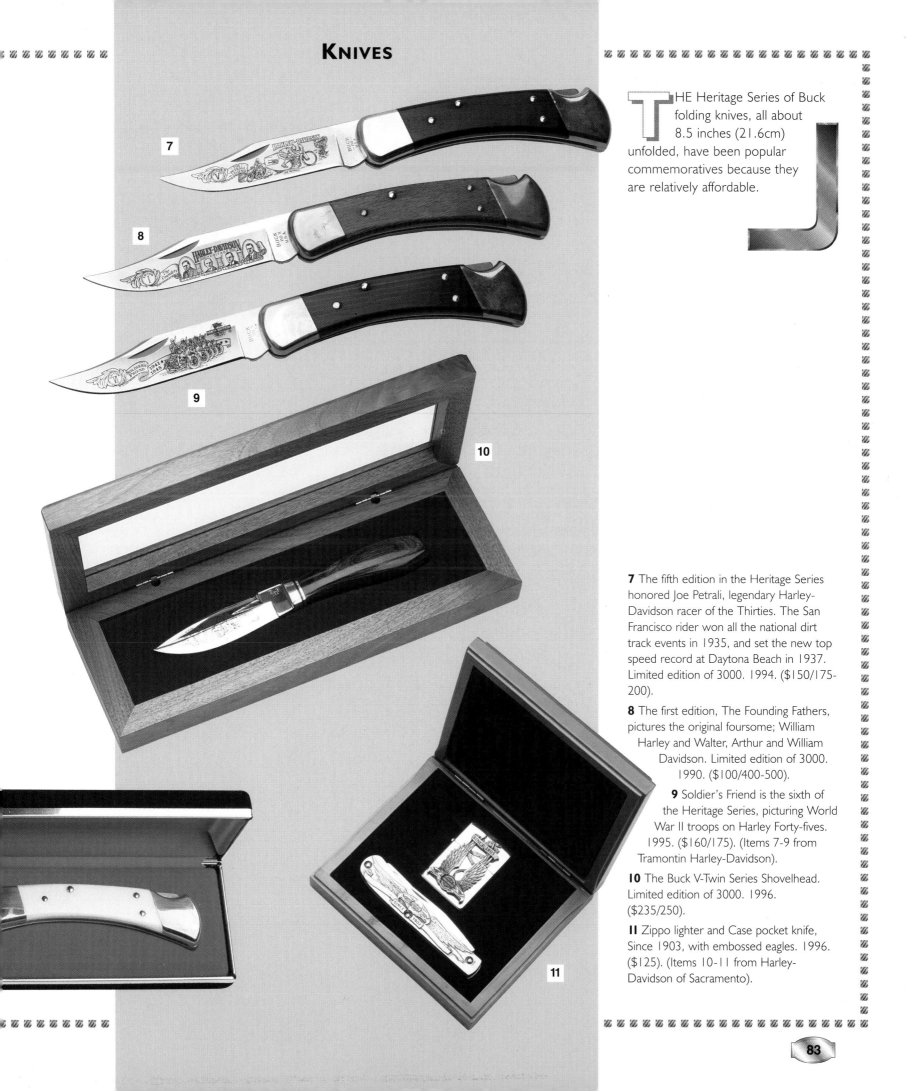

THE Heritage Series of Buck folding knives, all about 8.5 inches (21.6cm) unfolded, have been popular commemoratives because they are relatively affordable.

7 The fifth edition in the Heritage Series honored Joe Petrali, legendary Harley-Davidson racer of the Thirties. The San Francisco rider won all the national dirt track events in 1935, and set the new top speed record at Daytona Beach in 1937. Limited edition of 3000. 1994. ($150/175-200).

8 The first edition, The Founding Fathers, pictures the original foursome; William Harley and Walter, Arthur and William Davidson. Limited edition of 3000. 1990. ($100/400-500).

9 Soldier's Friend is the sixth of the Heritage Series, picturing World War II troops on Harley Forty-fives. 1995. ($160/175). (Items 7-9 from Tramontin Harley-Davidson).

10 The Buck V-Twin Series Shovelhead. Limited edition of 3000. 1996. ($235/250).

11 Zippo lighter and Case pocket knife, Since 1903, with embossed eagles. 1996. ($125). (Items 10-11 from Harley-Davidson of Sacramento).

RACING memorabilia provides a wealth of material for fans and collectors of Harley-Davidson competition history. Most of the more contemporary gear shown has been sold at special events to benefit charities.

1 Harley-Davidson factory rider Chris Carr's racing helmet, signed. Carr won the national championship in 1992. ($500-600). (Custom Chrome collection).

2 Factory rider Scott Parker's formal pit shirt, signed. This shirt carries added value for the racing number 2, which is one more than the digit most often worn by the seven-time national champion. ($200).

3 Parker's Alpine Star racing boots, slightly scuffed. ($200).

4 and **5** And Scott Parker's D's racing leathers, 1995, the year of his sixth national title. Milwaukee's orange and black competition colors have been dirt-track fixtures in American racing for more than 80 years. Should Parker win his eighth championship in 1997, he will have doubled the previous record. A feat not likely to be repeated. ($2500). (Items 2-5 from Wheels Through Time Museum).

EVERY Harley-Davidson dealership in the country has attracted a few fellows who liked to go racing. Not of few of whom were the shop owners.

6 The two-piece set of racing leathers worn by Ken Kraemer, a dirt-track racer of the Fifties. ($250).

7 and **8** Motorcycle racer Carl Doran of Robinsdale, Illinois competed in board track in the Twenties and dirt track in the Thirties and Forties. His early style kidney belt and football helmet show the scraped patina of racing and years. ($400). (Items 6-8 from Wheels Through Time Museum).

9 Harley-Davidson racing jersey from the Fifties, when nylon replaced cotton, which had supplanted wool in the manufacture of competition clothing. Leather and nylon, and subsequently polyester fabrics, became the foremost foundations in racing togs, and still are. ($150-200). (Dudley Perkins collection).

10 Armando Magri's dirt-track steel shoe, last used in competition in the Forties. ($ np). (Lu and Armando Magri collection).

RACING posters and race/win advertising have gone hand in hand since motorcycle racing began heating up in 1907. Most motorcycle dealerships and independent shops had walls covered with posters crowing about the latest racing victories.

1 In 1960 Brad Andres won his third 200-miler and led a Harley-Davidson sweep at Daytona. This was the final year for the fabled beach-road course, and the event moved to the Daytona International Speedway in 1961. ($50-100). (Lu and Armando Magri collection).

2 Joe Leonard was the American Motorcycle Association's first Grand National Champion based on points from the whole season. Previous national champs were winners of the annual 50-lap race on the Springfield Mile. Leonard won the title in 1954, 1956 and 1957, then became a successful car racer. Leonard's engine was built by San Jose tuner Tom Sifton. ($50-100).

3 In 1961 the annual Charity Newsies half-mile national championship was won by Carroll Resweber, in the process of winning his fourth straight Grand National Championship. Resweber had magic on the dirt track, and was the most naturally talented rider of his era. ($100-150). (Items 2-3 from Wheels Through Time Museum).

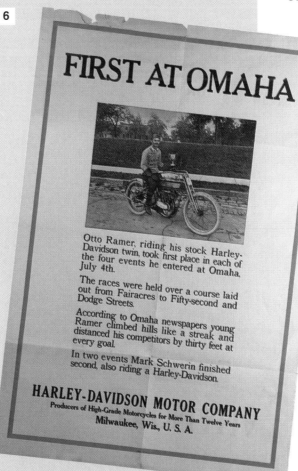

AMERICAN dirt track expanded in the Sixties and Seventies with a new generation of riders, and more manufacturers contesting Harley-Davidson for top honors.

4 Bart Markel, Grand National Champion in 1962, 1965 and 1966, recorded his record-breaking 28th national win at Columbus, Ohio in 1971. It was his final national victory. His successors in the "Michigan Mafia," Corky Keener, Rex Beauchamp and Jay Springsteen carried the banners thereafter. ($50-150). (Wheels Through Time Museum).

5 In the Thirties and Forties Armando Magri, of Sacramento, California, was a dirt-track specialist. He later became a Harley-Davidson dealer, a pioneering trail rider, and remains an active motorcyclist at his current age of 82. ($ np). (Lu and Armando Magri collection)

6 Harley-Davidson didn't have a full-scale factory racing team until 1915, but they were glad to advertise regional victories in amateur events around the country. ($1500).

7 Advertising posters have always provided an appealing format for graphic artists to portray the excitement of motrcycle racing. This poster, circa 1955, touts the Labor Day races at the Tulsa, Oklahoma fairgrounds. ($250). (Items 6-7 from Wheels Through Time Museum).

DALE Walksler's Wheels Through Time Museum is adjacent to his Harley-Davidson dealership in Mt. Vernon, Illinois. His collection of H-D memorabilia is one of the most comprehensive in the country, and is on display to the public.

1–5 The range of racing collectibles extends to early programs, direct mail advertising and event tickets. The flyer for the Los Angeles national hillclimb in the Twenties features a dramatic shot of a rider challenging the hill. The programs for the 1947 Illinois dirt track and 1952 Wisconsin race employed illustrations of the racers in action. ($75-100). Jim Clark's envelope advertising for the 1928 championship race in Wisconsin indicates the bold approach no doubt required of an Indian dealer in Milwaukee. The unused complimentary tickets and rain checks for a 1927 championship race have been well preserved. ($100-150).

6–8 These trophies from the Thirties and Forties were awarded to Harrison Reno, a California racer who was a compatriot of Armando Magri. One of Reno's race machines is displayed in the showroom of Harley-Davidson of Sacramento. ($300-400).

9 The program for the premier dirt-track race at Lancaster, Pennsylvania. ($50-100). (Items 1-9 from Wheels Through Time Museum).

By the Forties, American motorcycle racing had established an annual series of regional events throughout the country. The most popular and/or successful were usually national championship events.

It's the Greatest
THE FAMOUS
'COW BELL' CLASSIC
32nd ANNUAL
JACK PINE RUN
– NATIONAL CHAMPIONSHIP –
TOPS IN COMPETITION · ADVENTURE · THRILLS
Two-Day Endurance Run
500 Miles of Motorcycling You Will Never Forget
Sunday & Labor Day
August 31 – September 1

EXCLUSIVE TROPHIES FOR: A & B Solo & Sidecar, Club and Dealer Teams

Jack Piners Banquet Saturday Night

Timed by Longines-Wittnauer "World's Most Honored Watch"

Prizes:
IMPORTANT: All Entries Must Be Postmarked No Later Than August 24th

Lansing Motorcycle Club

10 Michigan's Jack Pine Enduro, also known as the Cow Bell Classic, is one of the longest-running and most prestigious off-road events in motorcycling. When the 500-mile enduro resumed after World War II, Claude Goulding, on a BSA 350, ended Harley-Davidson's consecutive win streak at 14. In 1953 Don Pink won the 27th Jack Pine on the new Harley KH. ($150-200).

11 The poster advertising the 1958 Jack Pine Enduro, hosted by the Lansing Motorcycle Club. As noted on the cow bell, the 1957 event went to Gerald McGovern on the new Harley-Davidson Sportster. ($200/250). (Items 10-11 from Wheels Through Time Museum).

12 This silver cup was awarded to John J. Cox in 1914, for winning the Tandem Motorcycle Division at the New York Commercial Tercentenary. Chances are he rode a Harley-Davidson. ($700-800). (Pat and Al Doerman collection).

13 and 14 The program for the annual Charity Newsies national in Columbus, Ohio in 1951 pictures previous winner Bill Tuman. The Richmond, Virginia half-mile national in 1968 went to Bart Markel, the first of five nationals he would win that year. ($75-100). (Wheels Through Time Museum).

THE world of automotive art had attracted a number of sculptors over the years, but there have been relatively few bronze artists working with motorcycle forms. More recently, the work of such craftsmen as Mark Patrick and Steven Posson has created more interest in the medium.

1 "The Reunion," by sculptor Mark Patrick, commemorates the 90th anniversary of Harley-Davidson in 1993. The maquette was produced in a limited edition of 1500. ($100/200-300). (The Shop collection).

2 The solid brass rendition of "The Reunion" was limited to 90 examples. Shown here is the artist's proof edition, before the numbered run was cast. ($2000/3500). (Wheels Through Time Museum).

3 This bronze statuette, issued in 1992, is inscribed with the expression, "If you can't run with the big dogs..." Limited edition of 1500. Artist and price unknown. (Custom Chrome collection).

METAL SCULPTURE

ALTHOUGH most of the artists modeling motorcycles worked in pewter, porcelain or bronze, gold and silver appeared in some pieces.

4 "The Drifter," another work by Mark Patrick was issued 1990, and this example was the first in a bronze edition of 100 dedicated to Barry Brown, a Canadian collector. ($2400/3500). (Wheels Through Time Museum).

5 This Shovelhead, crafted in silver, is pictured full scale. The 3-inch (7.62cm) model was made in Italy in the Eighties. Artist unknown. ($ np). (Lu and Armando Magri collection).

6 "Kick Start," by Mark Patrick was produced in 1989, and the bronze edition was limited to 35. Also dedicated to Barry Brown. The rider's love/hate relationship with his machine is well rendered. ($1600/2800). (Wheels Through Time Museum).

7 For its diamond anniversary in 1978, Harley-Davidson commissioned a scale replica of the 1903 model. The "American Spirit" was produced in volume in a metal version and in the limited edition of 145 renditions in sterling silver and gold, with inset diamonds in the pedals. The undertaking hit a snag when the makers realized the model could not be produced at the quoted price, and bailed out. Harley found another builder to fill the orders and avoided some embarassment. ($2700/14,000-16,000). (Dudley Perkins collection).

1903 Harley Davidson
Diamond Anniversary
of
America's Motorcycle

THE Eighties brought even more varieties to the forms and materials employed in the creation of motorcycle memorabilia and collectibles. Young artists began resurrecting many of the styles and methods of sculptors, potters, whittlers and toymakers of the increasingly distant past. With this variety came a growing selection in the market, and the inspiration for other artists to work with both mechanical and human figures.

1 The relaxed rider and his machine are cast in resin and hand painted. Some figures in this style have been misrepresented as unique pieces and sold at exorbitant prices. Artist unknown. ($50-150). (Bob Kovacs collection).

2 This ceramic figurine of a couple and bike was produced in 1989. Artist: Ken Lamonette. ($50-75). (Custom Chrome collection).

3 This hand-painted plaster statuette marked the 50th anniversary of the annual Black Hills Classic rally in Sturgis, South Dakota. Produced by Shade Tree Creations. 1990. ($50/100-150). (Bob Kovacs collection).

4 Wooden hog plaything for youngsters. Unknown origin. ($ unknown). (Custom Chrome collection).

5

6

7

8

9

AS Harley-Davidson's misfortune of the Seventies was transmogrified by its success in the Eighties, more independent representations of its products appeared on the market. Some were certified as official products, for a fee, by the company. Many more were not.

5 "The Wrench," by Mark Patrick was created in 1992. The painted version shown here, made of hydrostone, was produced as an edition of 500. ($154). The bronze edition was limited to a run of 20. ($1900/2500). (Custom Chrome collection).

6 This stylized wood model was made in France. Artist unknown ($ np). (Lu and Armando Magri collection).

7 Resin statuette, in the same style shown above left, measures 18 x 14 inches (46 x 36cm). Made in the Philippines, artist unknown. ($50-150). (Bob Kovacs collection).

8 Harley-Davidson touring bike as a woodie. Unknown origin. ($ np). (Custom Chrome collection).

9 This is a plastic kit model of a 1943 Harley-Davidson WLA military Forty-five. The combat patina and nearly barren setting were created by Dale Herd. ($ np). (Lu and Armando Magri collection).

N the mid-Eighties, Harley-Davidson intensified its program of trademark protection and official licensing efforts. As the brand name became more popular, and subsequently more profitable for vendors and Milwaukee as well, more official Harley-Davidson licensed products appeared for sale. Unlicensed vendors were discouraged from using any Harley-Davidson registered names or images.

1 The 1957 Sportster replicated in 1/10-scale by The Franklin Mint. The finely detailed die-cast models are made in China. 1995. ($150-175). (The Shop collection).

2 The 1980 Harley-Davidson FLT, combining die-cast metal and plastic, is 16 inches (41cm) long. The model was marketed in the Hammacher Schlemmer catalog. ($450/500-600). (Lu and Armando Magri collection).

3 The 1986 FXST Heritage Softail in a waving-flag display box. The 1/10-scale die-cast model was produced by the Franklin Mint in 1992. Made in China. ($140/200). (The Shop collection).

4 and **5** These two 1/10-scale die-cast models were issued by The Franklin Mint in 1995. The Police FLH ($110/135-160) and the 1976 Liberty Edition FLH ($150/175-200) were both hand-assembled in China. (Lu and Armando Magri collection).

SCALE MODELS AND REPLICAS

BY the Nineties, officially licensed Harley-Davidson models were being manufactured in China, Japan, Great Britain, the Netherlands, Italy and Germany, as well as the United States.

6 Harley-Davidson's return to roadracing is represented in this die-cast version of the VR-1000, made in China. 1995. ($75).

7 This ⅙-scale die-cast model of a 1979 Harley-Davidson Electra Glide dresser was made by Marvin International in 1992. ($400-500). (Items 6-7 from The Shop collection).

8 The most-seen Harley chopper in the world, "Captain America" from the 1970 motion picture "Easy Rider." The Franklin Mint die-cast model was issued in 1996. ($136/150-200). (Lu and Armando Magri collection).

9 The Harley-Davidson 1977 FXE Super Glide in a ⅙-scale plastic model by Tmiya-MRC, Japan. Made in 1986. ($100-150).

10 This ⅒-scale plastic model of the 1980 Harley-Davidson FLH 80 was produced by Academy-Minicraft in 1988. Made in Korea. ($42/50-100). (Items 9-10 from the Custom Chrome collection).

NOSTALGIA, becoming everything it used to be and then some, naturally evolved as a popular theme for porcelain figurines in the Nineties. These have all been commissioned as official Harley-Davidson products, and are sold in dealerships around the country and the world. Astute collectors generally buy two each, one to keep and the other for future sale as a valued memento.

1 "Twenty-Nine Days Til Christmas," a hand-painted porcelain maquette of Fifties young folks admiring the new 1957 Sportster. Based on the 1989 commemorative plate. Made in China. Limited edition of 3000 issued in 1994. ($170/200-250). (The Shop collection).

2 "Tree House Christening" is one of the ceramic figures in The Young Rider Series, which began in 1993. Issued in 1995. ($25/30). (Wheels Through Time Museum).

3 "Rural Delivery" was introduced in 1993 in a limited edition of 3000. ($125/150-200).

4 The "Joy of Giving" porcelain group was issued in 1991 in a limited edition of 1550 ($110/200-300). (Items 3-4 from the Lu and Armando Magri collection).

FIGURINES

5 and **6** Editions four and five of The Young Rider Series appeared in 1995. They were called "Harley Rides – 5 cents" and "The Engine Lesson." ($28). (Wheels Through Time Museum).

7 The official Harley-Davidson doorstop is porcelain Knucklehead and rider cruising along a country road. The 7-inch (18cm) tall figurine has a lead base and weighs 3 pounds (1.4kg). First issued in 1995. ($30). (Bob Kovacs collection).

8 "Harley-Davidson University" was issued in 1994 in a limited edition of 875. The assemblage includes pewter, wood, and porcelain. ($150-300). (Dudley Perkins collection).

9 and **10** The second and third editions in The Young Rider Series were "Free Wheelin'" in 1993 and "The Enthusiast" in 1994. ($25/30). (Bob Kovacs collection).

P ROBABLY the most popular and some of the most highly valued Harley-Davidson collectibles are the cast iron motorcycle toys of the Twenties through Forties. The early toys made of tin, lead, die-cast metals and plastic are also highly sought after.

1 and **2** The Champion Hardware Company was a prominent American manufacturer of cast iron toys in the Thirties. Their police motorcycles were generally made in large (7 inches, 17.8cm), medium (5 inches, 12.7cm) and small (3.5 inches, 8.9cm) formats. The smaller machines at the left are Harley-Davidson style, one with a battery-powered headlight. ($75-150). The larger models are patterned after the Indian motorcycle, with rubber tires on wood hubs. ($150-300). (Mark George collection).

3 This 1929 Harley JD with Parcel Post sidevan was made by another famous U.S. toymaker, the Hubley Manufacturing Company, in 1928. The 10-inch (25.4cm) toy was offered in olive green and red versions with a uniformed, detachable rider. The lights and handlebar were nickel-plated and the rubber tires rode on tin spoked wheels. This and the similar Traffic Car 3-wheeler are rare and valuable. ($2000-7500). (Pat and Al Doerman collection).

4 Motorcycle cop with swivel head, by Hubley, 1932. Made with both nickel-plated wheels/tires and tin spoked/rubber versions. ($500-1500). (Wheels Through Time Museum).

5–7 Champion models in three sizes; the 5-inch (12.7cm) police Harley at left has all rubber wheels/tires ($175-300); the 6-inch (15.2cm) Indian style of the same era has wood hubs ($250-400); the 3.5-inch (8.9cm) sidecar rig was the smallest model ($100-250). (Custom Chrome collection).

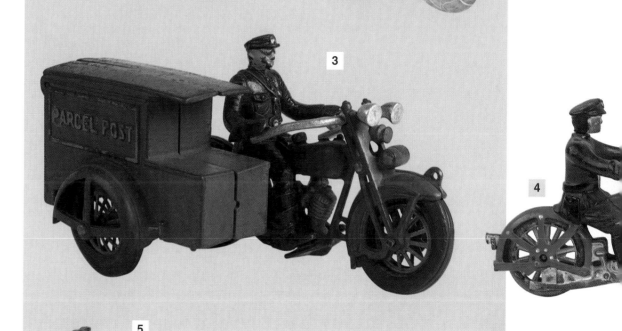

METAL TOYS

MANY of the early cast iron toys have been reproduced, and most are sold as contemporary renditions. Misrepresentation, however, is not unknown.

8 This large Champion police cycle and rider have been repainted, which generally subtracts from the market value. This is the Indian-style front end with rubber tires and wood hubs. ($250-500). (Lu and Armando Magri collection).

9 This Hubley Harley with a civilian rider was popular in the early Thirties. The 6-inch (15.2cm) model was offered in dark and light blue, green, orange and red. Some were made with wood hubs and others with tin spoked wheels. ($300-500). (Pat and Al Doerman collection).

10 Hubley's hillclimber, which also dates from the early Thirties, was a popular model and was produced in some volume. But not many survived their owners' racing habits. ($250-1200).

11 The red Indian-style patrol model was made by A.C. Williams in the Thirties. ($300-900). (Items 10-11 from Wheels Through Time Museum).

12 The red 4.5-inch (11.4cm) Hubley Crash Car was a product of the Thirties, and came with either rubber or nickel-plated tires. ($100-300).

13 The blue Special delivery trike was built in the Thirties by the Kilgore Toy Company, another U.S. manufacturer, and came in four colors. ($350-800).

14 Hubley's 5.5-inch (14cm) Popeye Spinach Wagon capitalized on the popular cartoon character. It dates from the late Thirties. ($400-1200). (Items 12-14 from the Mark George collection).

TIN wind-up and friction-motor toys were also enormously popular in the Twenties and Thirties. Like the cast iron toys, most were made in the U.S.A., Great Britain and Germany. In the Fifties most of the production switched to Japan, which manufactured millions of the colorful little novelties.

1 This friction motor monkey-clown toy was made in Japan by Rising Sun Trademark in 1950. The 5-inch long (12.7cm) toy produces a siren sound and the umbrella rotates in the monkey's hand. ($250-600).

2 The Atom stunt rider by Masudaya of Japan was produced in the early Sixties. This 12-inch (30.5cm) long battery-powered toy makes motor sounds, lights its headlight and has a stop/start function. The articulated rider swings his leg up and pivots as the cycle turns. ($750-1500). (Items 1-2 from the Custom Chrome collection).

3 This 16-inch (40.6cm) friction toy was manufactured by IY Metal Toys of Japan in the Fifties. ($2500-7000). (Wheels Through Time Museum).

4 The Patrol Auto-Tricycle by Nomura of Japan was made in the Fifties and Sixties. The 10-inch (25.4cm) long, battery-powered model has figure-8 mode, bump-and-go, a working headlight and whistling police-boy who steps on the "crutch pedal" (sic). ($250-750). (Bill's Custom Cycles).

5 The Circus Clown Motorcycle from Y.Y. of Japan is a Sixties' product. The 6-inch (15.2cm) long toy is spring-powered and makes a pivot U-turn. ($150-350). (Custom Chrome collection).

6 Plastic battery-powered roadracer built in Japan in the Sixties. The machine leans to one side on a stabilizer wheel and so moves in circles when turned on. Manufacturer unknown.($50-150). (Pat and Al Doerman collection).

7 This Harley-Davidson V-twin, trademarked TN/Auto Cycle, was manufactured by Nomura of Japan in the Sixties. The 9-inch (22.9cm) model has a friction motor and clear plastic cylinders to view the working pistons. ($300-600).

8 This curious Harley-Davidson inline 3-cylinder was also made by Nomura-TN/Auto Cycle in the Sixties. The 9-inch (22.9cm) toy has a friction motor that also powers the three open-air pistons. ($400-800).

9 A tin wind-up toy made in China. Manufacturer unknown ($ unknown).

10 The Police Squad toy was made by Louis Marx, U.S.A. in the Fifties. The 8.5-inch (21.6cm) wind-up is equipped with a siren. ($300-500).

11 A Police model made by the Unique Art Manufacturing Company, U.S.A. in the Thirties. ($300-500).

12 The small wind-up police models are both from the Thirties,and were both made by Louis Marx & Co, New York. ($100-300). (Items 7-12 from the Custom Chrome collection).

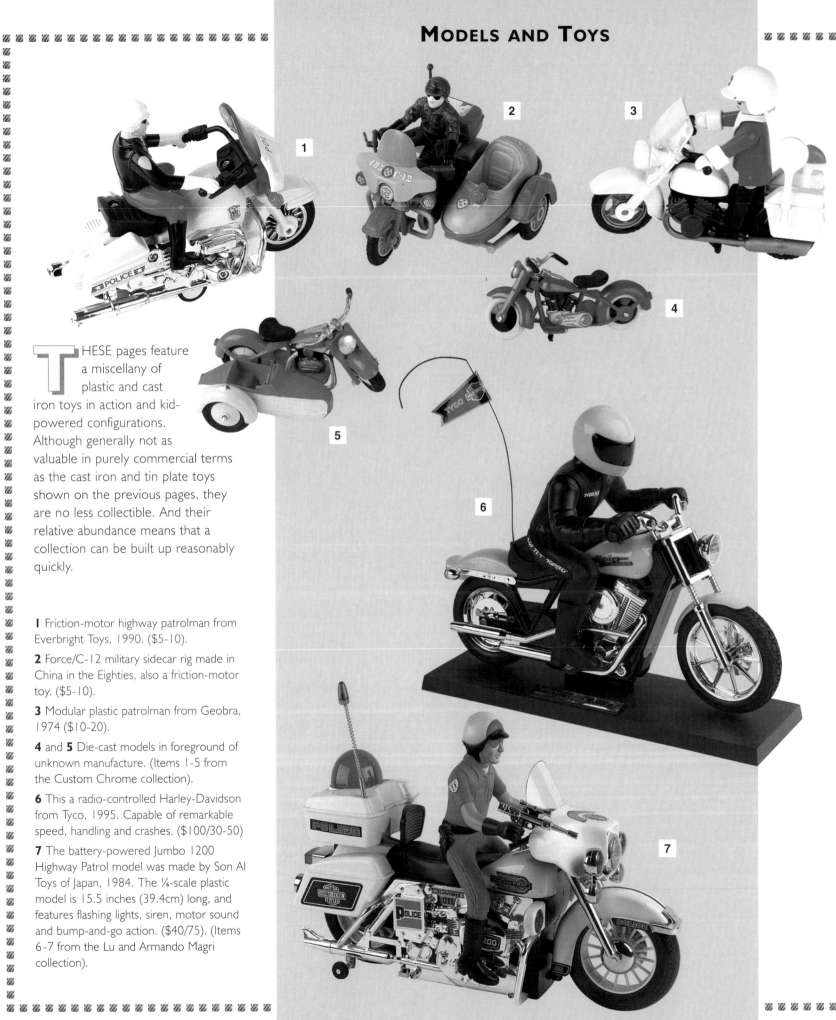

THESE pages feature a miscellany of plastic and cast iron toys in action and kid-powered configurations. Although generally not as valuable in purely commercial terms as the cast iron and tin plate toys shown on the previous pages, they are no less collectible. And their relative abundance means that a collection can be built up reasonably quickly.

1 Friction-motor highway patrolman from Everbright Toys, 1990. ($5-10).

2 Force/C-12 military sidecar rig made in China in the Eighties, also a friction-motor toy. ($5-10).

3 Modular plastic patrolman from Geobra, 1974 ($10-20).

4 and **5** Die-cast models in foreground of unknown manufacture. (Items 1-5 from the Custom Chrome collection).

6 This a radio-controlled Harley-Davidson from Tyco, 1995. Capable of remarkable speed, handling and crashes. ($100/30-50)

7 The battery-powered Jumbo 1200 Highway Patrol model was made by Son Ai Toys of Japan, 1984. The ⅙-scale plastic model is 15.5 inches (39.4cm) long, and features flashing lights, siren, motor sound and bump-and-go action. ($40/75). (Items 6-7 from the Lu and Armando Magri collection).

PLASTIC AND MOTORIZED TOYS

8 The Turbo Chopper is a battery-powered model with working lights and siren. Manufactured by Toy State, China, 1994. This is a nicely detailed model, right down to the dent in the tank. ($30-50).

9 The 9-inch (22.9cm) long plastic CHiPS higway patrol model with battery power made by Japanese manufacturer Bandai, 1977. The model has stabilizer wheels under the engine section. It was produced in association with the MGM television series. ($75-200). (Items 8-9 from the Lu and Armando Magri collection).

10 Large battery-powered plastic highway patrol model with lights and siren by MGH Toys of Korea. Year unknown. ($50-100).

11 Small plastic Hubley cop cycle from the Fifties. ($25-125).

12 Hubley Police Department cycle without rider. ($2-50).

13 The Evel Knievel stunt wind-up toy made by the Ideal Toy Co., Hollis, New York, 1972. Powered by a gyro motor, originally sold with Evel action figure. ($20-50).

14 Donald Duck pilots the Harley-Davidson Servi-Car. This 5-inch (12.7cm) long friction-motor toy of the Fifties was licensed by Walt Disney Productions. ($150-300).

15 Auburn police motorcycle, a 6-inch (15.2cm) plastic model from the Fifties. ($50-150).

16 Yellow wind-up model from Hong Kong, manufacturer and price unknown.

17 Harley-Davidson police model by U.S. maker Thomas Toys. This dates from the Fifties. ($50-100).

18 Die-cast police model by Matchbox, 1982. The bodywork combines metal and plastic. ($20-50). (Items 10-18 from the Custom Chrome collection).

BATTERY-POWERED toys for the kids, and coin banks (so they can save for a real Harley-Davidson), have attained collectible status in recent years. Again, most collectors buy two and leave one unopened in the original package, so that it remains in mint condition to appreciate in value as time passes.

1 Kenworth Sonic Hauler tractor-trailer rig by the Buddy L Corporation is battery-powered with audio from the engine, air brakes and back-up horn. 1994. ($60/100).

2 Harley-Davidson Semi-Trailer bank. The 1/64-scale metal model has a coin slot in the rear door. Edition of 50,000. 1994. ($48). (Items 1-2 from The Shop collection).

3 Motorized stunt cycle by Matchbox, Collector's Edition with patch and pins. A string attached to the rider's helmet spins the motor. 1991. ($12/20).

4 Matchbox Hog Riders Tour Bikes, die-cast models, for ages 3 and up. 1991. ($10/15-20).

5 Harley-Davidson Strobe Quadcycle, battery-powered sound and lights. Made by the Buddy L Corporation, China. 1993. ($25-30). (Items 3-5 from the Custom Chrome collection).

ALTHOUGH most of these toys are posted with minimum ages for younger owners, the average age of their owners is usually considerably higher. Few wives believe that these toys are actually intended for the children.

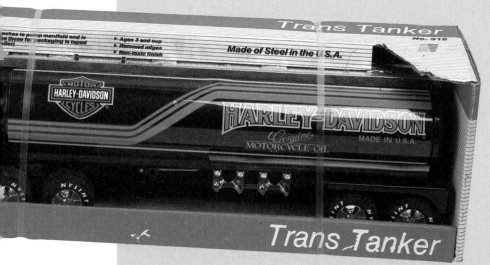

6 Matchbox Toys motorized Stunt Set for ages 4 and up. It includes a daredevil ramp, ring of fire loop and Harley-Davidson patch. The motor is operated by a pull-cord helmet. Die-cast metal and plastic. 1991. ($12/15-20).

7 Harley-Davidson Road Riders collector's set made by Matchbox Toys. It includes one die-cast tractor-trailer rig and one Low Rider motorcycle. Sold with either orange or blue bike. 1992. ($5/10-15).

8 Special Edition Harley-Davidson Sportster by Matchbox Toys. This die-cast metal ⅟₁₅-scale model features working fork, suspension and sidestand. It was sold with a display stand. Also available in Electra Glide versions, solo and sidecar. 1993. ($15/30-50). (Items 6-8 from The Shop collection).

9 The Harley-Davidson Trans Tanker by Nylint of Rockford, Illinois. "Made of Steel in the USA." This is a scale model of a Freightliner tractor and tanker with old-style factory lettering. For ages 3 and up. 1987. ($40/200-300). (Richard Callinan collection).

SCALE-MODEL kits in plastic figure in most boyhood enthusiasms, whether it's airplanes, ships, cars or motorcycles. Naturally enough, any such kits with a Harley connection have been rapidly absorbed into the world of "Harleyana."

1 The Eagle Express electric train set, 90th anniversary commemorative H.O. gauge set made in 1993. It includes an 8-wheel drive locomotive, two freight cars, tanker and 90th anniversary caboose. Oval track and power pack included. ($100/125-150). (Custom Chrome collection).

2 The Harley-Davidson Electric Racing set by Tyco. It includes two motorcycles, 13 feet (4m) of track and two hand-held controllers. Made in Hong Kong, Malaysia, China and USA in 1994 ($100/150-200).

3 Harley-Davidson 1979 FLH Sport 1/12-scale plastic model kit. A licensed product by Imex Model Co., Brooksville, Florida. Made in Japan. ($35/50-60). (Items 2-3 from the Bob Kovacs collection).

4 Harley-Davidson Duo-Glide plastic model kit by Ideal Toy Corporation, Hollis, New York. The 1/9-scale models were produced in the early Seventies; they were made in Japan. ($12/40-60). (Bill's Custom Cycles).

5 The 1980 AMF/Harley-Davidson FLHC Classic, 1/12-scale plastic model made by Imai of Japan in 1982. ($14/30-50). (Bob Kovacs collection).

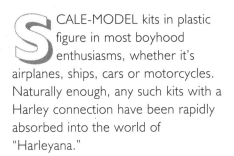

PLASTIC models gained popularity in the Seventies, as did the image of famous motorcycle distance jumper Evel Knievel. For a while, a veritable merchandising industry grew up around his exploits, as the items at the foot of this page amply demonstrate.

6 Early rider jigsaw puzzle in commemorative wood box, by Antique Cycle Supply, Cedar Springs, Michigan. The box contains a picture of a couple with 1930 UL model and sidecar. 1995). ($14/30-40). (Custom Chrome collection).

7 Rough Rider Shovelhead chopper by Revell, a 1/12-scale plastic model. This is the model prototype by Bob Kovacs. Made in 1971. ($8/75-100). (Bob Kovacs collection).

8 Early rider jigsaw puzzle by Antique Cycle Supply. The picture shows a rider on a 1916 Model J. 1995. ($14/30-40). (Custom Chrome collection).

9–11 A montage of Evel Knievelana. From the left: a plastic model kit by Addar Products of Brooklyn, New York. 1974. ($10/30-50).
A plastic model of Evel with a stunt bike by Ideal Toy Company, New York. 1972. ($4/10-20).
Evel Knievel Ring of Fire jigsaw puzzle by H-G Toys, Long Beach, New York. 1974. ($5/20-40).
Evel Knievel Thermos bottle by Aladdin Industries, Nashville, Tennessee. 1974. ($4/10-30).

12 Evel Knievel, King of the Stuntmen mask and costume by Ben Cooper Inc., Brooklyn, New York. 1974. ($12/30-50).

13 Evel Knievel metal lunchbox, featuring the semi-legendary Snake River Canyon jet-cycle jump. Aladdin Industries, Nashville, Tennessee. 1974. ($6/15-50). (Items 9-13 from Wheels Through Time Museum).

THE Harley-Davidson die-cast coin bank series, inaugurated in 1989, has grown steadily as a popular collectible for kids and adults, mostly the latter. The banks vary broadly in terms of collectible value, since some were issued in limited editions from 500 to 3000, but most were produced in much greater numbers.

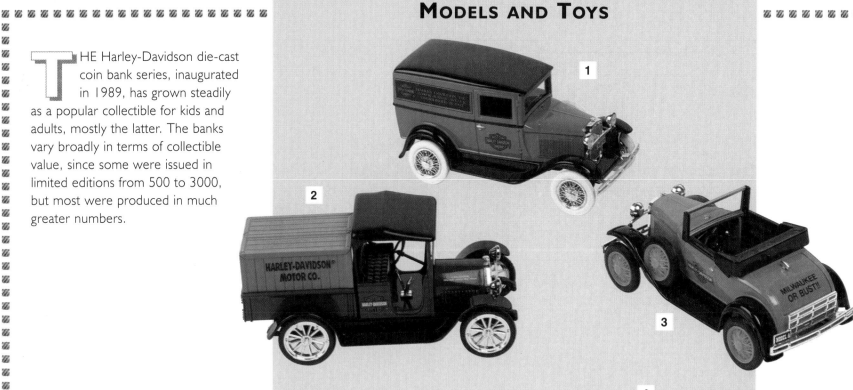

1 The 1931 Ford Model A delivery van by Liberty Classics issued in 1993. ($37/60).

2 1918 Studebaker pickup truck also from Liberty Classics. 1995. ($40/50).

3 1929 Ford Model A roadster. 1993. ($30/100) (Items 1-3 from The Shop collection).

4 1955 Chevrolet Cameo pickup truck, ⅟₄₃-scale by Ertl Company, Dyersville, Iowa. 1996. ($20). (Tramontin Harley-Davidson).

5 The first installment in the Harley-Davidson coin bank series, the 1918 Ford Runabout, a limited editon of 5088. 1989. ($18/600-750). (Richard Callinan collection).

6 1913 Ford Model T van dime bank. 1994. ($18/25).

7 1930 Chevrolet delivery truck dime bank. 1994. ($18/25). (Items 6-7 from Tramontin Harley-Davidson).

COIN BANKS

8

9

10

11

12

13

14

AS two of the banks on this page prove, some of these coin banks have become quite valuable because of their rarity. It is ironic that you would now need to spend hundreds of dollars to buy a bank that is supposed to encourage the habit of saving.

8 The 1931 Hawkeye tanker bank was produced as an edition of 7500 in 1992. When demand outran supply, another 504 were manufactured without the Limited Edition inscription. Ironically, the second run is now the most valuable. ($26/#1:200, #2:600). (The Shop collection).

9 The 1936 Dodge tanker truck with Refinery Sealed Oil. 1996. ($39). (Custom Chrome collection).

10 1932 Ford custom sedan delivery bank. 1994.($18/25). (The Shop collection).

11 1940 Ford woody station wagon bank, number 6 in the Ertl series. 1994. ($25).

12 1951 GMC panel delivery bank. 1994. ($25).

13 1932 Ford panel truck bank. Edition of 5232,1991. ($22/250-350). (Items 11-13 from Tramontin Harley-Davidson).

14 The 1926 Mack Bull Dog truck bank was the second one in the series. It was produced as a limited edition of 5016 in 1990, and runs a close second to the Ford Runabout in collectible status and value. ($19/500-700). (Richard Callinan collection).

BANKING on the future, Harley-Davidson has maintained a steady presence in the savings business. Encouraging youngsters to save for the real motorcycle, or hog, of their dreams is made easier when the money goes right into a miniature version of the goal. Of course, most of these banks reside on the desks or bookshelves of grown-ups, who may still cultivate the same dreams. Big boys who can now afford big toys, or hope that they soon will. Or women, of course, who were determined to buy their own machines, or who married the right big boys.

1 The Horse & Wagon coin bank was offered as a limited edtition of 5000 in 1991. ($25/125-150). (The Shop collection).

2 and **3** The 1931 Civilian and Police Servi-Car models were produced in 1996. The Police model includes handcuffs and nightstick. ($59). (Harley-Davidson of Sacramento).

4 and **5** The Gold and Silver Anniversary hog piggy banks both appeared in 1985. The banks are gold and silver plated, with removable gas caps. ($100/500-700). (Custom Chrome collection).

THE two pieces at the top of this page show that not all of the Harley-Davidson banking series took the forms of wagons, trucks, cars or motorcycles.

6 This Harley-Davidson oil can bank was produced in the early Sixties as a dealer advertising premium. ($50-100). (Pat and Al Doerman collection).

7 The First Factory replica was issued as a porcelain coin bank in 1984. ($20/300-400).

8 and **9** The 1933 Motorcycle Sidecar bank is a 1/12-scale die-cast model with steerable fork and rubber tires. The one-year-only stylized eagle tank graphic is hand-painted. The 1994 banks were produced in limited editions of 3000 each. Gold finish on a marble base. ($235/500-600). Silver finish on a walnut base. ($60/100-200). (Items 7-9 from the Richard Callinan collection).

10 and **11** The 1933 sidecar model bank was also built in an edition of 40,000, painted in black and red with gold striping. ($60). (The Shop collection).

ANOTHER long-running standard in the Harley-Davidson catalog of functional memorabilia is the watch, both wrist and pocket. This page features a miscellany of Harley-Davidson watches from over the years.

1 This timepiece was produced for Harley-Davidson in the early Sixties, using the traditional bar and shield emblem. ($25-50). (Pat and Al Doerman collection).

2 A more contemporary rendition of the bar and shield appear on this ladies' watch presented as a dealer award in the Seventies. ($150-200).

3 Gold-plated watch from 1976, with Harley-Davidson Number 1 logo as the second hand. ($100-150). (Items 2-3 from the Lu and Armando Magri collection).

4 Illinois Watch Co., circa 1915. ($400-500).

5 Silver engraved Elgin watch from about 1920. ($400-500).

6 Another Illinois watch with engraved gold case and brushed face, 1924. ($400-500).

7 A Swiss-made gold watch commemorating the Black Hills Motor Classic in South Dakota, no date. ($300-400).

8 Gold engraved watch with bar and shield, circa 1915. ($400-500).

9 Elgin gold pocket watch, circa 1929. ($400-500).

10 Gold pocket watch by Waltham with bar and shield emblem, probably from the early Fifties. ($400-500).

11 and **12** This 1994 V-Twin Power wrist watch featured an illustration of the 1915 F model, sold in an oil can case. ($75/80-100).

13 The 90th Anniversary Reunion pocket watch was issued in 1993. ($140/300-400). (Items 4-13 from the Custom Chrome collection).

WATCHES

TIMEPIECES are timeless ways of preserving memories from specific times and places. Even though the watch mechanisms may no longer function, the style and craftsmanship carries the imagery of time marching on.

14 This Swiss-made Biker Fob Pocket watch was produced in 1994. Made of stainless steel, and with a water resistant case, it can be worn on a belt or with an attached chain. Available in black or brown leather. ($95). (Custom Chrome collection).

15 More contemporary wristwatches from Harley-Davidson Motorclothes, sold in embossed tin Panhead cases. The face features an illustration of an old fashioned oil can graphic. Offered in both men's and ladies' sizes. 1994. ($75). (Bob Kovacs collection).

16 Engraved silver Gruen wristwatch, circa 1930 ($250-300). (Mark George collection).

17 Witnauer wristwatch with bar and shield, circa 1946. ($100-150).

18 Men's version of watches shown in figure 14. 1994. ($75). (Items 17-18 from the Bob Kovacs collection).

19 A well-worn gold-plated pocket watch with bar and shield, circa 1920s. ($250-400). (Mark George collection).

MANY enthusiasts will say you can have the time of your life on a Harley-Davidson, so it follows that Harley-Davidson clocks would figure prominently in collections comprised largely of pieces of time. Most of these wall clocks were originally manufactured as advertising tools for dealers only. Now modern reproductions have recreated the styles of past eras, and many are sold in Harley-Davidson dealerships.

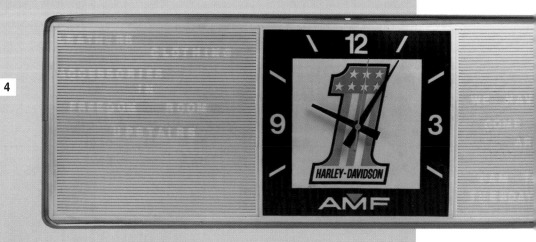

1 Harley-Davidson dealership clock, circa 1949. ($3000-3500). (Wheels Through Time Museum).

2 Contemporary Harley-Davidson wall clock with chrome and neon framework. ($325). (Farrow's Harley-Davidson).

3 Harley-Davidson dealer clock with bar and shield emblem, 1947. Manufactured by Neon Products, Lima, Ohio. ($1000-2500). (Wheels Through Time Museum).

4 AMF/Harley-Davidson wall clock/bulletin board from the Seventies. Approximately five feet (1.5m) wide. Made by Dualite, Inc., Williamsburg, Ohio. ($500-600). (Richard Callinan collection).

5

6

7

THESE clocks are definitely contemporary beneath the surface, but displaying the design and styling touches of the Thirties, Forties and Fifties. Harley-Davidson recognizes that the traditional styles of the past have lasting appeal, and help reinforce the company's proud representation of its history.

5 Official Harley-Davidson dealership wall clock of the Eighties, when the Retro styling was revitalized for corporate identity. ($250-300). (Richard Callinan collection).

6 This 1984 wall clock is another example of design nostalgia in terms of graphics and styling. The louvered outer disc rotates. ($500-600). (Farrow's Harley-Davidson).

7 Contemporary Harley-Davidson neon clock with vintage racing action illustration. Nearly 18 inches (46cm) in diameter, this clock is sold in Harley dealerships. 1996. ($1000). (Farrow's Harley-Davidson).

COLLECTIBLE timepieces or pieces of time. These pages display some of the wide range of wall clocks, grandfather clocks and custom pieces that bear the Harley-Davidson name.

1–3 Contemporary Harley-Davidson wall clocks with vintage graphics from the Thirties and Forties. Battery-powered. 1996. ($22). (Harley-Davidson of Sacramento).

4 The grandfather-style oak School House clock was produced in 1983. ($190/250-300).

5 Lighted wall clock produced in 1988; battery-operated. ($150-200). (Items 4-5 from the Richard Callinan collection).

6 Official Hamsters clock. The Hamsters Motorcycle Club is composed of business people in the motorcycle trades who are connected indirectly with Harley-Davidson. The name was chosen to reflect the carefree, relatively harmless and generally cute nature of the members. ($50-75). (Bob Kovacs collection).

7 Wall clock and handmade collage of watch parts by David of London, owned by Magri of Sacramento. 1983. ($125-175).

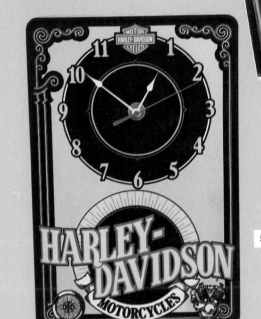
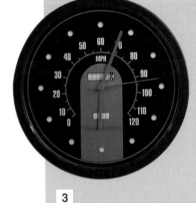

LIKE clockwork, the design and manufacture of clocks continues to tick onward in style and fashion. These clocks remind us that it's time to ride.

8 Another framed wall clock and an assemblage of watch parts arranged to produce a 1938 Harley-Davidson Seventy-Four. Made by Ken Broadbent, Worcestershire, England. ($175-200).

9 A battery-powered desk clock, manufacturer unknown. ($75-100). (Items 8-9 from the Custom Chrome collection).

10 The neon bar and shield wall clock was produced in 1991. ($300/350-400). (Richard Callinan collection).

11 The Power Cruiser alarm clock awakens slumberers to the sound of a motorcycle engine, which is similar to the Harley-Davidson rumble. Year and price unknown. (Custom Chrome collection).

HARLEY-DAVIDSON, originating in Milwaukee, brewing capital of the USA, can naturally lay claim to a legitimate connection with the beer industry. Many of Harley-Davidson's early family, management and labor, were beer drinkers. As were many more of their customers, past and present. Cheers.

1–4 Commemorative beers for the annual Black Hills Motor Classic, held each August in Sturgis, South Dakota. Shown are the cans for 1989, 90, 92 and 94. ($3-10). (The Shop collection).

5 Harley-Davidson V-twin beer poster made by H&M Enterprises, 1993. ($25-35). (Tom Brannan collection).

6 Unopened six-packs of Harley-Davidson beer, brewed by one of the several brewers in Milwaukee, are naturally more highly valued. This is the Daytona vintage. ($20-75).

7 and **8** 1989 and 1990 Daytona Heavy Beer (no viscosity indicated). ($4-6).

9–12 The annual brews for 1985 through 1988. ($5-10). (Items 6-12 from the Mark George collection).

BEER AND WINE

SPECIAL beers and wines have become part of national, regional and even international Harley-Davidson special occasions.

13 Another version of the Sturgis 50th Anniversary commemorative brew, 1990. ($4-5).

14 The Miller Genuine Draft memorial tall can produced for the Harley-Davidson's 90th Anniversary celebration in 1993. ($15-20). (Items 13-14 from Tramontin Harley-Davidson).

15 In the Eighties, Harley-Davidson succumbed to the yuppie invasion and sanctioned a wine cooler, produced by Scooter Juice of Santa Rosa, California. ($15-20). (Pat and Al Doerman collection).

16 Commerative brew from the Harley-Davidson Club of Denmark, 1986. An Odense Pilsner produced by Albani Bryggerierne. ($40).

17 Harley-Davidson beer with old-style oil can label; "% allowed for cling." Manufacturer unknown. ($20-30). (Items 16-17 from the Custom Chrome collection).

18 Special bottling of Healdsburg chardonnay, 1992. This was produced in celebration of Dudley Perkins Company's 80th anniversary. One of 80 bottles. Also offered in a cabernet sauvignon. Healdsburg, California. ($150-200). (Dudley Perkins collection).

FOR the more serious fan of distilled spirits, and collectors of American folk art, there are special edition whiskey decanters.

1 This commemorative eagle decanter was issued by Jim Beam in 1983. (Sealed, $59/250-300); (empty, $150-200). (Harley-Davidson of Sacramento).

2 The Eagle Soars Alone, Harley-Davidson decanter celebrating the company's return to private ownership, 1985. Limited edition of 3000. Brookfield Collectors guild, made in Germany. ($60/150-200).

3 Salute to America, produced in 1985 in a limited edition of 3000. Porcelain stein with pewter eagle. ($90/200-250).

4 Special decanter of Old Mr. Boston Bourbon, honoring the 36th annual edition of the Black Hills Motor Classic. Royal Halburton China. 1976. ($175-250). (Items 2-4 from the Custom Chrome collection).

5 The Harley-Davidson 85th Anniversary decanter, issued in 1987 in a limited edition of 3000. Porcelain with pewter eagle. ($100/150-200).

6 A Uniquely American Institution, pewter decanter of 1988 in limited edition of 2000. Brookfield, made by Gertz of Germany. ($100/150-200).

7 Flathead and Knucklehead shot glasses, pewter badges. 1992/93. ($12/15). (Items 5-7 from the Dudley Perkins collection).

DECANTERS AND STEINS

THER items of barware also celebrate the Harley-Davidson name. Germanic influences prevail in some of huge, ornately decorated steins for the discerning beer drinker.

8 Harley-Davidson bar spinner and bottle opener, made in 1932. ($150-300). (Wheels Through Time Museum).

9 A huge porcelain stein issued in 1993 by Gertz of Germany. Limited edition of 6100. ($130/150-175).

10 The V-Twin, An American Tradition, by Brookfield Collectors Guild. The stein portrays the evolution of Harley's V-Twin engine. The center panel reproduces the cover of the 1919 catalog. Made in Germany. Limited edition of 3000. 1985. ($90/200-250). (Items 9-10 from Harley-Davidson of Sacramento).

11 Pewter stein, A Uniquely American Institution, Brookfield Collectors Guild. It shows William Harley and Arthur Davidson working on the first 1903 Harley-Davidson motorcycle. Made in Germany, 1988. Limited edition of 2000. ($150/200-250).

12 The 80th Anniversary porcelain stein with pewter eagle head lid. It depicts the founders, the first factory and landmark motorcycles. Limited edition of 5000. Brookfield, made in Germany, 1983. ($85/$200-300).

13 Bar serving tray, Evolution V2 Revolution. 14-inch (36cm) diameter with cork insert, 1984. ($15/30-50).

14-17 The Oil Can bar set was produced in 1984. The ensemble included the pitcher, four mugs and four tumblers. ($40/100-150). (Items 11-17 from the Custom Chrome collection).

"SMOKIN' and drinkin', stayin' out all night, just livin' in a fool's paradise." as Mose Allison sang. Or was it drinkin' and gamblin'? Maybe all of the above, because they just seem to go together, in watering holes from the local tavern to the rowdy biker bar on the other side of town.

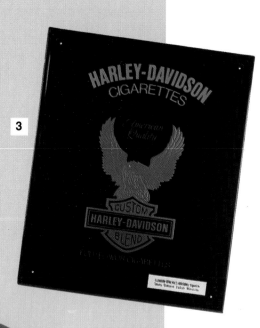

1 and **2** World War II and World War I commemorative lighters in brass. 1989. ($19).

3 Harley-Davidson Cigarettes, embossed tin sign. 1987. ($100-300). (Items 1-3 from the Custom Chrome collection).

4 Vinyl cigarette holder of the Fifites, favored by young ladies who smoked in style. ($10-25). (Pat and Al Doerman collection).

5–7 Daytona Beach commemorative ashtrays from 1957 and 1958, and plain stamped ashtray for the mechanics. ($10-20).

8 Harley-Davidson Zippo lighters from the late Eighties and early Nineties. From left: Harley-Davidson fuel tank nameplates from 1957, 1959, generic bar and shield art, Jack Daniels whiskey label Harley style, and a Harley-Davidson racing logo. ($15-35). (Items 5-8 from the Custom Chrome collection).

NOT long after the latest of these tobacco products were released, Harley-Davidson decided to get out of the cigarette business. That was just prior to the rush of lawsuits against tobacco companies. Timing is everything.

9 and **10** Harley-Davidson touring bike lighters; at left is a die-cast metal Electra-Glide, circa 1971, with a burnished finish. On the right is an enameled cast iron Tour Glide from about a decade later. Manufacturer unknown, both made in Japan. ($25-50). (Lu and Armando Magri collection).

11 Small matchbox in oil can design, made for Harley-Davidson by the Diamond Match Company of Milwaukee in the Sixties. ($15-25). (Bill's Custom Cycles).

12 A Harley-Davidson dealer promotion lighter from the Sixties, with enameled Panhead illustration. ($15-30). (Lu and Armando Magri collection).

13 The Harley-Davidson tobacco promotion package expanded in 1987, with a free nylon sport bag with the purchase of a carton. ($40-50).

14 A carton of Harley-Davidson full flavor cigarettes. ($40-50).

15 Buy-one-get-one-free twin pack of full flavor smokes. ($5-10).

16 Harley-Davidson Custom Quality American Blend lights, with promo packs for Daytona Bike Week '93. ($50-60).

17 Free Scripto butane lighter with the purchase of a package of cigarettes. ($30-40). (Items 13-17 from the Custom Chrome collection).

HARLEY-DAVIDSON, always searching for new formats to generate exposure for the coporate identity, recognized that candies and cookies were traditional favorites throughout the country. And the containers presented the company logo to more females who may well be potential customers.

1 and **2** Contemporary hand-painted gumball machines by Bob Kovacs. 1996. ($35). (Bob Kovacs collection).

3 Salt water taffy box as the original factory. Patsy's Candies, Colorado Springs, 1995. ($5-15).

4 Tin candy box with pewter 1929 Harley-Davidson JD insignia. Patsy's Candies. ($20-30). (Items 3-4 from the Dudley Perkins collection).

5 At left is the Hog Cookie Jar with the old-fashioned company logo dating from 1919. It was issued in 1984. ($35/100-150) The large hog piggy bank features the tank graphic from 1933. 1987. ($35/100-150). (Richard Callinan collection).

FROM beer and cigarettes to coffee and chocolates, Harley-Davidson managed to cover nearly everyone's favorite something. Promotional emphasis soon shifted to more domestic products such as music boxes, Christmas ornaments, wrapping paper and greeting cards. Milwaukee recognized early on that motorcycling was a family pastime, and that all members of the family were potential riders. This expansion of the company's non-motorcycle product line was first reflected by the increase in production of women's clothing and accessories.

6 Harley-Davidson Premium Chocolates, manufacturer and date unknown. Contents missing. The same box is shown open on the right. 1985. ($8/35-75 full, $10-20 empty)

7 A coffee maker in the style of the Genuine Harley-Davidson factory sealed oil can. It brews 30 cups, made by West Bend of Wisconsin, 1987. ($70/200-250).

8 Harley-Davidson genuine American-blend coffee, from Thomas Coffee Co., St. Louis, Missouri. ($5-10). (Items 6-8 from the Custom Chrome collection).

PORTABLE radios gained wide popularity in the Sixties, and were soon followed by small cassette players and smaller radios with better reception and improved sound reproduction. Harley-Davidson tested the market with small AM radios representing various company products.

1 Transistor radio in the style of a Harley-Davidson oil can, made in 1978. ($13/50). (Pat and Al Doerman collection).

2 A similar radio based on a Power Blend oil can with a photograph of a Shovelhead engine. 1979. ($13/50). (Richard Callinan collection).

3 Harley-Davidson fuel tank AM/FM radio. PF Products, China. 1995. ($50/60-75). (Bob Kovacs collection).

4 Contemporary Harley-Davidson Daytona AM/FM/cassette portable. PF Products, China. 1996. ($105). (Harley-Davidson of Sacramento).

5 Harley-Davidson Nostalgia wood-case radio. Thomas Collectors Edition, made in Hong Kong. 1986. ($125/200-250). (Richard Callinan collection).

HARLEY-DAVIDSON has continued to develop and expand its accessory line in the communications media. Telephones have been cleverly diguised as oil cans, beer cans, fuel tanks and complete motorcycles. Portable radios and tape players are cast in the industrial arts imagery of motorcycle engines.

6 Contemporary Harley-Davidson Venice Beach personal cassette player with belt. ($40). (Harley-Davidson of Sacramento).

7 Harley-Davidson 1994 FLSTC Heritage Softail Classic push-button telephone. Handset housed in the seat/tank assembly. 1994. ($50). (Fred Lange collection).

8 The Harley-Davidson Nashville, AM/FM/cassette portable. PF Products, made in China. 1996. ($95). (Harley-Davidson of Sacramento).

9 Harley-Davidson beer can telephone. Made in Hong Kong. 1986. ($30/50-100). (Custom Chrome collection).

THE Christmas season became a popular setting for Harley-Davidson nostalgia in the Eighties. The Christmas plate series was immediately successful, and remains in annual production nine years later. Note how the illustration styles changed over the years. Snow globes, some with music boxes, also appeared for the holiday celebrations.

1 The First Factory, this snow dome/music box was produced in 1989. The wind-up music box plays "Jingle Bells." ($20/200-250). (Custom Chrome collection).

2 The seventh issue in the Christmas plate series, Rural Delivery. Limited edition of 8500, 1990. ($35/60-100).

3 The Skating Party was the eighth Christmas plate, also an edition of 8500, produced in 1991. ($35/50-70).

4 The 1985 Christmas plate was titled The Perfect Tree. This was the second plate in the series, issued in a limited edition of 3000. ($23/600-700). (Items 2-4 from the Lu and Armando Magri collection).

PLATES AND SNOW DOMES

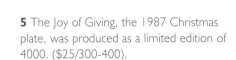

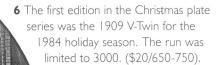

COLLECTOR plates have seen generous growth in dollar values over the years, and naturally the early numbers command the highest prices. Condition counts heavily with the plates, since some that have been openly displayed and exposed to considerable light have a tendency to fade. Many are kept boxed and put up only for the holiday season.

5 The Joy of Giving, the 1987 Christmas plate, was produced as a limited edition of 4000. ($25/300-400).

6 The first edition in the Christmas plate series was the 1909 V-Twin for the 1984 holiday season. The run was limited to 3000. ($20/650-750).

7 Number six in the series was 29 Days Til Christmas for 1989. This was made in a run of 5000, as the editions grew less limited. ($30/200-250). (Items 5-7 from the Richard Callinan collection).

8 Mainstreet USA was the third issue of Christmas plates, an edition of 3000 for 1986. ($25/450-550).

9 Santa's Secret, the Christmas snow dome of 1990. ($20/60-100). (Items 8-9 from the Lu and Armando Magri collection).

HARLEY-DAVIDSON has some experience with ornamentation, so it was hardly surprising when they began offering Christmas tree ornaments to brighten up the festive season.

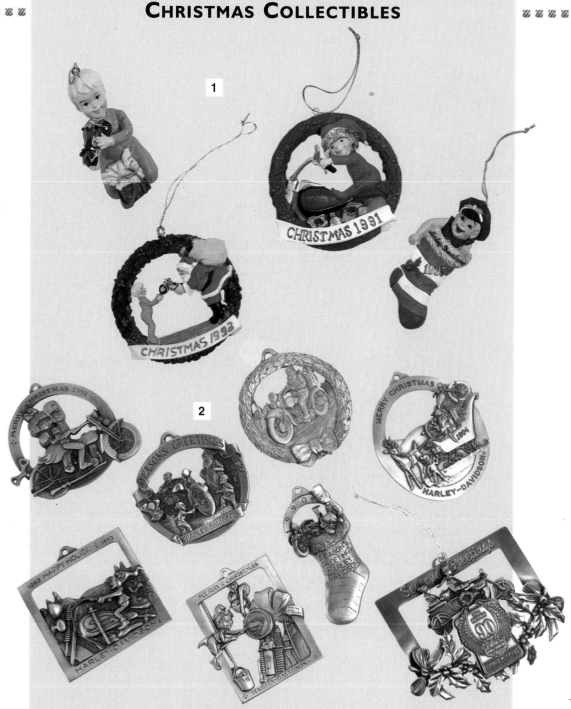

1 Plaster Christmas tree ornaments for children, from left:
First Harley, 1993. ($15/25).
The Gift was the series' second ornament, 1992. ($15/30).
Young at Heart was the first in the children's series, 1991. ($15/50).
Baby rider in stocking, 1995. ($15).

2 Pewter Christmas tree ornaments were first issued in 1988.
Top row, left to right:
Batteries Not Included, 1992. ($12/20-30).
Santa's Workshop, 1989. ($7/100-150).
Santa's Secret, the first edition in the pewter series, 1988. ($7/220-250).
Cleared For Takeoff, 1994. ($14/15-20).
Bottom row, left:
Joy Ride, 1993. ($12/15-20).
Finishing Touches, 1991. ($11/50-60).
Stocking Stuffer, 1990. ($9/75-100).
90th Anniversary Reunion ornament, 1993. ($12/15-20).

3 The annual Holiday Bulb Ornament serries, from left: 1987, 1988, 1989, 1990, 1991, 1992. ($6-8/10-20). (Items 1-3 from the Richard Callinan collection).

4

5

6

N addition to Christmas ornaments that were commercially available, Harley-Davidson also issued some especially to their dealers. A selection of these are shown on this page.

4 Above are Holiday Bulb ornaments from earlier years. From left: 1982, 1983, 1984, 1985, 1986. ($4-6/25-50). (Richard Callinan collection).

5 A miscellany of Christmas ornaments presented annually to Harley-Davidson dealers, including a Harley Owners Group ornament from 1994 at the upper left. Adjacent are stained glass ornaments for the 80th Anniversary in 1983, and the vintage lettering logo for 1985. ($50-100). Center row, left to right: 1994 padlock ornament. ($50-75).
1991 sparkplug decoration. ($50-75). Brass finish Santa, year unknown. ($ unknown). Stained glass-style with eagle, 1979. ($75-100).
Bottom row, left to right: 1988, 1990, 1993, 1989. ($50-75). (Dudley Perkins collection).

6 Dealer Christmas ornament from 1978, celebrating the 75th Anniversary, and pewter decoration from 1980. ($100-150). (Richard Callinan collection).

CHRISTMAS cards have not been overlooked in Harley-Davidson's comprehensive catalog of holiday commemorations. The motorcycling spirit oftens calls for reinforcement in the winter months.

1

2

3

4

5

6

1 Hog bank Santa Claus with mini hog bank reindeer.

2 A Christmas card from Willie G. Davidson to the Magris, 1985. It features a print of a Willie G. drawing of Carroll Resweber, Grand National Champion, 1958-61.

3 Unidentified Christmas card.

4 Winter scene with large hog bank.

5 Another Willie G. Christmas card, from 1984. It is a print of his painting of the original 1903 company shed/factory, 1963.

6 Christmas card with Santa as flat track racer. Illustration by Hector Cademartori. (Items 1-6 from the Lu and Armando Magri collection).

THE factory commissions its own cards for corporate use and others for sale to the public. Milwaukee also licenses independent publishers to use the Harley-Davidson logo. Licensed publishers generally commission freelance artists to create artwork for the cards. One of the most popular illustrators is Hector Cademartori.

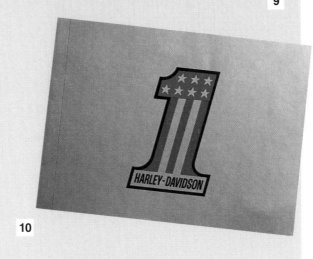

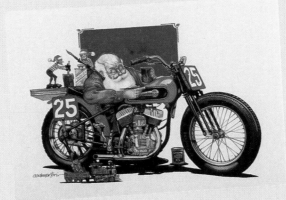

7 Fold-out Christmas card from the factory, mid-Seventies.

8 Santa on his Fat Boy being passed by a reindeer.

9 Winter scene with trike, illustration by David Mann.

10 Number One logo Christmas card from the Seventies.

11 Santa finishing up his WR dirt track racer. Illustration by Hector Cademartori. (Items 7-11 from the Lu and Armando Magri collection).

Note: Collector values on unused factory cards usually run from five to thirty dollars. Some illustrations are the same as those used on the Christmas plates.

ERE is a miscellany of Harley-Davidson memorabilia, based on no particular theme. The diversity of objects illustrated shows how huge is the range of collectibles that have grown up around the Motor Company's name.

1 Official Harley-Davidson dart board, tournament-quality bristle, fade-resistant graphics. 1994. ($65). Official Harley-Davidson darts, brass with anodized aluminum shaft, steel tip. Set of three. 1995. ($24). (Harley-Davidson of Sacramento).

2 Official Harley-Davidson waste basket with old-style oil can label. 20 inches (51cm) high. 1984. ($20/50-100). (Lu and Armando Magri collection).

3 Genuine Harley-Davidson battery stand and charger. ($150-300). (Bill's Custom Cycles).

4 Harley-Davidson jukebox by Rock-Ola. Vintage styling with hand-stained wood trim. Die-cast metal trim triple-plated with copper, nickel and chrome. Magazine holds 100 compact discs. 63 inches (160cm) high. 1994. ($7995).

5 Harley-Davidson limited edition acoustic guitar by Gibson/Montana. The bar and shield inlays on the headstock and neck are mother-of-pearl. The guitar top is made of Sitka spruce, and the back and sides of flame maple, with an Indian rosewood fingerboard. Limited to 1500 instruments. 1995. ($2500/2800-3000). (Items 4-5 from the Custom Chrome collection).

THE range of Harley-Davidson memorabilia runs from the pedestrian shoe wiper shown below to the stratospheric Stratocaster in chrome and gold. Something for every budget.

6 Oil can bar lamp, brass-plated hardware with glass globe. 1988. ($40/150-200).

7 Tiffany-style lamp with simulated leaded glass shade in plastic. Designed with swivel neck for use as either a table or wall lamp. 1975. ($29/150-200). (Items 6-7 from the Richard Callinan collection).

8 Harley-Davidson electric guitar, a Fender Custom Stratocaster. Chromed body with gold plated trim. Limited editon of 109. 1993. ($7000/16,000-19,000). (Harley-Davidson of Sacramento).

9 Hand-painted custom mailbox by Bob Kovacs. 1996. ($45).

10 Harley-Davidson Genuine vinyl welcome mat. 1990. ($25/30). (Items 9-10 from the Bob Kovacs collection).

MORE miscellany from Milwaukee and beyond. From stuffed animals for children to pillows for grown-ups, the Harley-Davidson emblem covers the spectrum. Even to the portable fishing rod for Dad.

1 Harley-Davidson plastic tackle box. ($18).

2 Harley-Davidson retractable fishing rod and reel by Shakespeare, Columbia, South Carolina. Made in China. 1996. ($49). (Items 1-2 from Harley-Davidson of Sacramento).

3 Wood motorcycle with sidecar music box, plays "King of the Road." Die Musik Box, Leavenworth, Kansas. ($ unknown).

4 Harley-Davidson teddy bear. R. Dakin & Co., San Francisco. 1984. ($20/30-50).

5 Pillow with an embroidered cover featuring 1930 advertising art. Date unknown, but probably from the early Eighties. ($25-50). (Items 3-5 from the Lu and Armando Magri collection).

MISCELLANY

As you can see in the vintage slide viewer pictured below, Harley-Davidson was an advertising-oriented company from its earliest days in the market.

6 Framed metalwork of 1903 Harley-Davidson, by Philippe Michaud, Cerritos, California. 1977. ($125/250-400).

7 Harley-Davidson stuffed eagle. R. Dakin & Company, San Francisco. 1984. ($20/35-50). (Items 6-7 from the Lu and Armando Magri collection).

8 Bar poker dice set with cup. The bar and shield logo represents the aces on the dice. 1985. ($13/40-50). (Custom Chrome collection).

9 The Magic Lantern slide viewer which dates from the Twenties. Harley-Davidson promotional glass slides are from the William L. Novotny dealership in Iowa City, Iowa. ($400-450). (Wheels Through Time Museum).

MORE coin banks, this time on the wing... And a further dip into the deep well of Harley collectibles.

1 The third edition in the Harley-Davidson vintage aircraft bank series. Produced as an edition of 21,696. 1993. ($38/60-100).

2 The first example in the plane series. Issued in an edition of 10,000. 1992. ($30/300-400).

3 The second of the airplane banks, built in a run of 25,000. 1993. ($30/100-150). (Items 1-3 from The Shop collection).

4 Harley-Davidson international commemorative stamp collection. It features mint stamps from Antigua, Bulgaria, Hungary, Mexico, the Turks and Caicos Islands and Sierra Leone mounted in a rosewood frame. 1994. ($160). (Tramontin Harley-Davidson).

5 Electric Speed Classic motorcycle racing game, by J. Pressman, New York. It probably dates from the Thirties. ($200-400). (Wheels Through Time Museum).

6 Carved wooden eagle. Artist, year and price unknown. (Harley-Davidson of Sacramento).

7 Vega model McDonnell-Douglas F-16 jet airplane by Liberty Classics of Libertyville, Illinois. Edition of 30,000, made in China. 1995. ($50). (Tramontin Harley-Davidson).

MISCELLANY

OUR guided tour of Harley-Davidson memorabilia, collectibles, mementos, keepsakes, knick-knacks, toys, antiques, commemorative issues, artwork and artifacts ends here. But... "the road goes on forever, and the party never ends."

8 Harley-Davidson ladies' handbag in the style of a saddlebag. Official Milwaukee product of the Fifties. ($100-200). (Pat and Al Doerman collection).

9 Harley-Davidson shaving kit with mug and brush, by the Franklin Toiletry Company. 1988. ($30/40-50).

10 Dudley Perkins Company of San Francisco paper clip.

11 Motorcycle key ring.

12 Dudley Perkins paper clips of the Seventies.

13 Dudley Perkins promotion tape measure. (Items 9-13 from the Dudley Perkins collection).

14 Ceramic figurine, Salute to America, with pewter emblem. Produced in 1986 by the Brookfield Collectors Guild, Milwaukee. Limited edition of 3000. ($190/800-1000). (Harley-Davidson of Sacramento).

15 The Harley-Davidson U.S. Special Delivery stamp collection. A framed collection of commemorative stamps, 1990. ($90).

16 Disposable 35mm camera, made in Japan. ($25-30). (Items 15-16 from the Custom Chrome collection).

CREDITS

Our thanks to the owners of these collections, for offering them for photography, providing the facts and figures, and for letting us play with their toys.

Thanks to Dale Walksler and his Wheels through Time Museum; Nace Panzica and Steve Davey at Custom Chrome; Tom Perkins of the Dudley Perkins Company; Pat and Al Doerman at Farrow's Harley-Davidson; Lu and Armando Magri and Harley-Davidson of Sacramento; Dave Hansen at The Shop; Robert Tramontin of Tramontin Harley-Davidson; Bill at Bill's Custom Cycles; Rich Callinan, Mark George, Brian "Bob" Kovacs and Tom Brannan.

We also acknowledge the authors and publishers of the works used as references: *Antique and Contemporary Motorcycle Toys* by Sally Gibson-Downs and Christine Gentry, (Collector Books, 1995); *Motorcycle Collectibles* by Leila Dunbar, (Schiffer Publishing, Ltd, 1996); *Nero's Price Guide to Harley-Davidson & Motorcycle-Related Memorabilia* by Bill Oren with Skip Peters, (Nero Enterprises, Inc., 1995), and *Scotty's Pictorial Motorcycle Toy Price Guide* by Scott Johnson, (Scott Johnson, 1996).

The author also extends his appreciation to editor Philip de Ste. Croix, designer Jill Coote and photographer Neil Sutherland, whose combined efforts made this a much better book than seemed possible at the outset.